THE
WAGON

CHICAGO VISIONS AND REVISIONS

*Edited by Carlo Rotella, Bill Savage,
Carl Smith, and Robert B. Stepto*

THE
WAGON
AND
OTHER
STORIES
FROM
THE CITY

MARTIN
PREIB

The University of Chicago Press

Chicago and London

MARTIN PREIB is an officer with the Chicago
Police Department. His essays have appeared in the
Virginia Quarterly Review and *Tin House.*

An earlier version of the chapter "The Wagon"
originally appeared in the *Virginia Quarterly Review.*

The University of Chicago Press, Chicago 60637
The University of Chicago Press, Ltd., London
© 2010 by Martin Preib
All rights reserved. Published 2010
Printed in the United States of America

19 18 17 16 15 14 13 12 11 10   2 3 4 5

ISBN-13: 978-0-226-67980-8 (cloth)
ISBN-10: 0-226-67980-2 (cloth)

Library of Congress Cataloging-in-Publication Data

Preib, Martin.
  The wagon and other stories from the city / Martin
Preib.
     p.   cm. — (Chicago visions and revisions)
   ISBN-13: 978-0-226-67980-8 (cloth: alk. paper)
   ISBN-10: 0-226-67980-2 (cloth: alk. paper)
     1. Preib, Martin. 2. Police—Illinois—Chicago.
3. Chicago (Ill.)—Social conditions. I. Title. II. Series:
Chicago visions and revisions.
  F548.54.P745A3   2010
  977.3'11—dc22   2009036010

This book is dedicated to my mother,
who loved the city she could never return to.

It is also dedicated to my friend, editor,
and adviser, Rob Keast, whose crucial support
and guidance never wavered, not once.

Listen! I will be honest with you;
I do not offer the old smooth prizes
But offer rough new prizes . . .

WALT WHITMAN
"Song of the Open Road"

CONTENTS

BODY
BAGS

The sergeant handed me a large clear plastic bag from the top of a file cabinet outside the commander's office.

"This will be a good experience for you," he said.

The bag was wrapped tightly in binding cords and was heavy. I alternately cradled it in front of my stomach and hoisted it on my shoulder. I did not know what it was, or what the sergeant meant. It was my second day out of the Chicago Police Academy. My partner, who would be training me that day, was late. I had no radio. I never heard the assignment about a removal, and, even if I had, I wouldn't know what it meant. Remove who? Where? Why? Rather than look stupid, I nodded and stood off to the side of the hallway after the sergeant left, not making eye contact with any supervisors in white shirts who might approach me and ask me who I was and what I was doing. I looked at myself, standing in the hallway with a large plastic bag cradled in front of me, without knowing why. I imagined my voice responding feebly to any inquiries.

"I really don't know."

After my partner showed up and informed me I would be driving the wagon in downtown rush-hour traffic, he directed me to a café for his coffee, obviously in no hurry to reach our assignment. The brief narrative on the computer explained that a woman was dead, and removal meant we must take her to the morgue. The narrative stated she was in her fifties. That was it. My partner did not speak about the task ahead, though I could not stop thinking about it. The service entrance to the address of our assignment, a high-rise building on Michigan Avenue, was below in the labyrinth of alleys and parking lots off Lower Wacker Drive.

I had never driven a wagon in traffic. I made my way there slowly, constantly stealing glances through the large mirrors on both sides, bracing myself for a collision each time I changed lanes, squeezing my head into my shoulders every time a bike messenger whizzed by, waiting for the slap of his body on the metal of the wagon. After we descended the ramp connecting the surface with Lower Wacker Drive, we roamed the back entrances of buildings looking for the address, but never found it. Many times I had to back up the wagon in tight turns between delivery trucks or concrete braces. A few times we were called on the radio and asked when we would get there. My partner told them to hold on, we were looking for the service entrance, but he didn't really seem to care. Then we both chuckled about giving up and just carrying the body out in a bag through the main entrance onto Michigan Avenue in rush hour.

Pardon me, body coming through. Look out.

Even as I was engaged in my first removal, I fought the image of myself doing it. I conceived of the police job as my first real career at the age of forty. Instead, hauling a dead body hinted at my life before the police, where I ended up in service jobs, mostly as a doorman hauling bags, while I entertained and pursued, fruitlessly, other plans: teaching, trying to oust the old guard in union elections, and writing. With the security of a police job, I had told myself, I could continue wandering the city, keep writing, and live decently. I could buy nice cars, go out to eat when I wanted, go on vacations to tropical islands. I imagined the more glorious aspects of the job. Everyone does. You are filled with this imagery in the academy: catching murderers and gangbangers, working together with other units in stings, becoming a detective, getting promotions. Hauling dead bodies was rarely mentioned, mostly because the labor was canceled in the last union contract and was slowly being phased out, district by district. The sergeant's statement echoed in my mind.

Good for me?

Eventually a Latino maintenance man was sent to the entrance to flag us down. An elevator we never noticed before opened, and he walked out, waving at us. I parked the wagon as close as I could, and we walked into the building, the maintenance guy leading the way. My partner reminded me of the bag, and I went back to retrieve it, its purpose clearer now. The halls were dimly lit, the paint thick. It was a well-kept building, but old, requiring steady care. One could sense the many layers of paint on the walls and trim. We rode the small elevator together, not saying anything. When it opened, I smelled death for the first time. The question that had been lingering since we got the job now came to the forefront: Could I handle this? If I failed to complete this task, I feared I would never live it down. Would I be ostracized? My spirits plummeted; the smell was so awful.

I recalled somebody once told me to inhale through my mouth and exhale out my nose at the scene of a dead body. Two detectives stood down the hallway with gloves on. The door to the apartment, the obvious source of the smell, was held open by a small rug. On the floor they had measuring tape, clipboards with notes attached. As we walked closer, the smell intensified, so that when I walked into the dark room after we spoke to the detectives, I became a little dizzy. I looked down on the floor next to the bed at the woman wrapped up in blankets, only part of her face and her hair visible. I would learn later that a dead body wrapped up in blankets is usually a good break. All you had to do was carry the body with the blankets into the bag. Sometimes you never even had to touch them, just roll them into the bag. But since the cause of her death was still unknown, we had to unwrap her for investigation.

At my partner's direction, I set the bag next to her and tugged on the plastic binding, but could not open it. He whipped out a knife from his vest pocket and handed it over to me. The bag expanded out onto the floor of the apartment after I cut into it. He grabbed the outer, clear plastic and pushed it over to the side. It was garbage now. We took the remaining black bag and spread it next to the body, unzipping it all the way. I positioned myself at her feet and slowly tugged on the blanket, which was stuck to her decayed skin. I turned my head away from her. My partner said I needed more force. I pulled harder and she unwrapped, her decayed skin ripping from the blanket noisily. She rolled out onto the floor, much of her skin and face purple and green. Clumps of hair stuck to the blanket, the smell billowing out of the now-exposed body and secretions on the floor, the blanket, and her clothes. I turned my head. I became dizzier, left my position, and walked to the open window, pulling in clean air and dry heaving.

The detectives looked at me, then my partner.

"His first one, second day on the streets," my partner said.

They nodded and after they inspected her for any signs of foul play, the elder detective took my position and pushed her skillfully into the bag. I stood next to him. I never even touched her. They had no obligation to look out for me. Nothing else was said about it.

Somewhat ashamed at my inability to do the job, I now overcompensated. I grabbed the bag by the handles on the sides and slid her down the smooth carpeting of the hallway by myself, into the service elevator, and out to the wagon, where we each took a side and lifted her in. We pulled off our gloves and threw them in the Dumpster. Then I awkwardly maneuvered the wagon out of the narrow loading zone, back and forth at least six times, the reverse alarm sounding each time I shifted, and we ascended back to the surface of the city with our body bag in the back, my partner sipping his coffee.

Writing about Chicago poses a formal dilemma. On the one hand, I carried a heavy duty that obliged me not only to collect the messy remains of failed life and intent, and all its attendant baggage, but also to make sense of it, meaning out of it. Until that answer arrived, I was pulled downward by my experiences in the city, my need to know it, all the while craving the form that would let me transcend it. There is no more wrongheaded state of mind. I had no idea where I was going, but, in retrospect, I think this confusion serves a purpose: No one thinking clearly would keep going. I did not move in a straight line; rather there were stops and starts, rejections of the enterprise, then returns to it. Often, in the self-accounting that takes place when I recalled these experiences, these stops and starts were the most debilitating signs of what I conceived as my failure and my wasted life.

Let me be more specific. Capturing a place like Chicago poses a challenge because the various devices of nonfiction and fiction both fall short. Since the aim of writing about place is to illuminate it, not escape or transform it, I felt constrained to facts and realism. Yet I always sensed something more lingered behind them, particularly in Chicago, whose ambivalence to truth and fact is well known. To get there, I was drawn to the mechanisms of fiction. But it was my own experience in the city I wanted to capture, not an imagined character. In this condition, all forms, tenses, and points of view danced in front of me, canceling each other out, each one holding possibilities, each one showing its obvious insufficiency as it was written.

Nevertheless, a faith lingers, a faith that this desire to write about place will one day reveal the appropriate form. This form, unreachable for so long, seems to come all at once, unifying elements like point of view, tense, and substance. But there are, in fact, preludes with distant roots, recognized clearly only in retrospect. These preludes provide their own narrative, so I went back to them. A religious force moves to the forefront, unifying the writing. I passed through many intellectual and artistic "schools of thought": moral, didactic, political, from realism to romanticism, before I realized that what I was seeking was not necessarily a definable place, subject, or theme, but the appropriate understanding of a mystery, rooted in the city, that had drawn me in all along, a mystery that was alive and provided satisfaction these other forms could only partly, and therefore insufficiently, satisfy. Much of what could be called my "voice," I concluded, was the manner in which I would approach this mystery. I saw that not only does this mystery survive my lowest sinking; it intensifies along the way, undeniable evidence in my mind that the mystery is real.

In retrospect, I wondered at how long I fought the context of this mystery, partly from my own cowardice, partly in deference to current literary pretenses. Here my education proved destructive. It tended to pull me away from the base and unorthodox corners where I lingered, where I often preferred to go. Rather than embrace these places, I tried to escape them, seek other sources deemed more noble and appropriate. I got lost in schools, art scenes, planned trips to Europe, writers' workshops, repressing the sense that what was in front of me was already more compelling.

One bitterly cold day on the far north side of Rogers Park, I was assigned a removal in the basement of a large apartment building. I stood off to the side while another officer, Jimmy, finished his report and waited for the detectives to call back and declare, officially, no further investigation was required. I moved to the back of the basement, to the warmest section, holding a conversation with Jimmy but aware that, try as I might, I could not keep my attention away from the body in the corner, partially under the couch, as if the dead man had crawled under it. He was about the sixth body that month. I had had enough of them. I was sick of working the wagon, sick of Rogers Park with all its various dead, more dead than any other district I had worked. How could they make cops, wearing uniforms with ties, stoop to such labor, I groused. When it came time to turn him into the bag, I stopped, stood there. I could barely tolerate the job anymore. Only a sense of duty pushed me onward. Jimmy, with some fifteen years on the job, seeing my hesitation, taunted me good-naturedly, then walked over and pulled the body into the bag with an ungloved hand. Show-off. My partner and I lifted, bearing the body out the door and down the gangway into the brutally cold, bright winter day. The light reflecting off the snow contrasted with the dark basement, causing us to squint. We had to stop to rest three or four times; the body weighed about 275 pounds.

I looked at myself resting on the thin sidewalk between two buildings, the black bag on the ground between us, glanced at my partner across the alley.

Here in this gangway, I admitted a writer willfully loses his sense of direction, finds repose in an imagery that exudes its own music, one in which issues of form, fact, and fiction find their own resolution. Piety prevents me from dissecting this imagery further, dissection being, as they say, a fancy word for murder. My concern now was its life span, durability, and my ability to remain in it. What most terrified me, thrilled me, was not the resolution of form, but its hint of the divine, lingering, like an elegy, among what is lost and what remains.

THE
WAGON

The dead seek the lowest places in Chicago: We find them in basements, laundry rooms, on floors next to couches, sticking out of two parked cars or shrubs next to the sidewalk. It is more than gravity that pulls them down, for in every dead body there is something more willfully downward: the lowest possible place, the head sunken into the chest and turned toward the floor.

No matter the cause—an accident, a murder, or, as we cite on the Hospitalization Case Report, natural causes—all bodies express this downwardness when we remove them from the cavern they have created merely by their presence, by their being.

Some cops, like me, circle the periphery of the room before we encounter the body, making small talk with other cops guarding the scene, slowly putting on our gloves, unnecessarily double-checking that our path is clear, anything to avoid the inevitable bending over the body and touching it, shaking it from this descendance it insists upon and bringing it back into our living world, where it must be pronounced, photographed, identified, prodded, stripped, and categorized.

Their resistance is powerful. The dead roll back to their original positions, stuck to the ground or their sheets on their beds, their bodies unwilling to bend or sway into the bag, always pulling themselves back down, a force captured in the phrase "dead weight."

I am glad to have a partner who forces the issue. He positions the large diesel wagon as close to the site as possible and wordlessly takes off his radio, rolls up his sleeves, and tucks in his shirt. He grabs the body bag and the gloves from the truck. He marches into the building or crime scene and holds open the bag with a leg or arm while the rest of his body is spent maneuvering it in. I shake myself free from my limbo and jump to assistance. I take my side, and we work together until we can get the bag around the body and zip it up, communicating in short statements, ". . . his arm . . . watch the head . . . he's leaking there." My partner never wants to double-bag the dead as I do, dreading the fluid drips that in the smallest amount will ruin a uniform. Instead, he grabs the bag by the handles, lifts, and heads back to the truck.

"I just want to get it over with," he says after we get back into the front seats and begin driving to the morgue. He is polite, acknowledging and explaining the reasons for his taking control, the sign of a good partner.

"Oh yeah, sure, no problem. Me too," I say, letting him know I am glad he did.

The drive to the Near West Side can take forty-five minutes and is a welcome break. We listen to calls on the radio, look at beautiful women, and keep our hands away from our faces, fearing that despite our best efforts, some small remnant of the dead is on us. We remind ourselves to use extra soap and some kind of fragrance when we wash our uniform that night. Even so, we sense the dead person in the back of the wagon as if we are keeping a secret, and we are. None of the people with whom we make eye contact as we drive have any idea there is a dead body in the back of our wagon.

Even when we open the door to the wagon at the morgue, the dead seemed to have burrowed deeper into it, and again they fight us when we slide them out onto the gurney, though it is much easier to handle them now that they are in a bag. The gurney fits the level of the wagon floor exactly. All we have to do is pull on the handles and the body slides out.

At the morgue the dead grow more sullen, insisting on remaining in the same awkward positions they were in when they died, positions we would find impossible to endure. They will be faced upward in a well-lit room, the body bag suddenly and rudely opened with a razor and any clothes or blankets cut away. My partner and I stand on the other side of a window watching the attendant process the dead, the unforgettable smell of the dead battling the smell of disinfectants spread liberally on the walls and floors. The morgue attendant weighs them, measures them, and removes their possessions and records them on the form, which we must sign. It means reentering the room where there are often several other bodies waiting further processing. We use the morgue pen: Until we can scrub our hands, we will touch nothing that will come with us. The cavalier conversation among the morgue attendant, cops, and funeral directors can only intensify the ignominy of the dead. They will remain in this morgue under constant bright lights for a few days, until the funeral home is ready to remove them.

I often think what wisdom and honesty there is in the fact that we bury the dead. It strikes me as the single truthful element of the process. After the humiliation and rudeness of being disturbed from their dying place by the police, left in the constant fluorescent light of the morgue, what a relief to be placed deep into the dirt. Perhaps we are forgiven after we sink the dead into the dirt for disturbing them at their place of death, for putting them through this legal and social process. Perhaps we are forgiven for disguising the dead to look like the living at the funeral and blathering about resurrection over them.

No hard feelings, right?

The dead do not lack the means of descending by themselves. To us their labor is slow and offensive, but in time, if left to their own devices, the dead can descend into any death place. Their secretions leak out onto the bed or the ground, and their flesh hangs lower. It will sag from their bones. Their face will cave in and secretions flow from the anus or any other openings, everything immediately downward, so thoroughly deep into the place of their death that nothing can get the scent out. It is clear to me that the dead do not want us near them, for the stench they emit after four or five days is so offensive to every living thing—save the maggots who feed on them—that you will never forget it. What a travesty, I think, what false religion, to cremate them and send their ashes billowing haphazardly about our world, strewn about our roads, stores, churches, cars, as if they haven't told us clearly in their death position where they want to go.

For this there can be no forgiveness.

For most of the day, I avoided the crime scene of the murdered Macedonian man. Instead I questioned residents of the apartment building as they came and went. I even found a witness who had exited the elevator in the lobby around the time of death. He heard moaning and signs of a struggle coming from the laundry room. He hesitated, and then left the building.

I only stared at him silently when he asked me, "You don't think I let him die, do you?"

The dead man was in the laundry room, down a few steps from the lobby, on the floor facedown, his head bashed on the side and his face bloody and swollen. The head was tucked into the floor with patches of blood next to him and on the wall, and we only saw the gaping wound when we pulled him up and rolled him over. The murder weapon, a fire extinguisher, was already taken by the detectives. The man was part of a group of Macedonian immigrants who landed jobs as property caretakers for real estate companies. Known for their reliability, they are given apartments and small salaries to run the daily operations of rental buildings until they save enough to buy their own two-flat. Everything about the man indicated struggle: an immigrant, a menial job, old clothes, a building mixed with students, menial workers, and a few young professionals.

I prefer to cover the dead with shrouds to avoid seeing the wounds or touching their flesh and having their secretions touch me. I find the fresh white shroud a welcome contrast to the death scene. There is something holy in their cleanliness and their whiteness and in the word "shroud." I do not think the dead mind it either, for it provides some cover from the living, like the curtains around a hospital bed.

My regular partner hates this delay and often rejects it, but today I have a different partner, Todd, and I am in charge. Todd has a reputation for avoiding the darker police duties, and I perceive these rumors are accurate. Several weeks ago he completed a case report on a dead person when my regular partner and I arrived. There was also an older sergeant there near retirement. Without saying anything, the sergeant grabbed a section of the body bag barehanded and helped us carry it out to the wagon while Todd just stood by and watched the three of us, an act that immediately and categorically condemned him in all our eyes. Even now he is standing away, letting me get the body ready and hoping I will take the position at the head, where the body oozes secretions from the wound. I conclude I will never willingly ride with this partner again. After that day when he avoided his duty in carrying the dead, his endless chatter about real estate deals, investments, and the salary his lawyer girlfriend earns makes him all but unbearable. Only on the third try did the dead Macedonian man roll over, me near his head, Todd at his feet, so we could push him into the bag.

I have witnessed enough of the life struggle preceding death to know that death is resisted with a superhuman and terrifying strength. The man shot in the leg with blood pouring out raises himself up, only encouraging the flow of blood, not restricting it.

Car crash victims often flail violently as they get closer to death, ignoring the burden these desperate acts place on their already diminished life resources. When my mother suffered a cardiac arrest, she lay still for a moment as her face swelled and turned blue and I begged her not to leave me. Then with a strength I did not believe she possessed at her age, she pulled herself up to me three times in wild convulsions, putting her face next to mine and squeezing, begging, I am certain, for me to help her, though I could do nothing. Then she lay still until my cousin breathed new life into her, and she came rushing back.

But I see a different conviction in the dead. I see the dead no longer bearing weight the way the living do, but impressed by it, unrelentingly so. I know there comes a point in dying when a person realizes they have failed their life struggle. One failure often brings to life all others, their aggregate weight unbearable. Perhaps our failures are the last images of our life, the most powerful this new weight of failing life itself, but right behind it all the others, imposing that desire to crawl into some hole we felt after we remembered our inability to become what we imagined, how much we hurt someone we loved, how we squandered our life or just failed to understand it, or how we fell short so many times. Did the Macedonian man realize this as he lay on the concrete floor of the building? Did he suddenly see his whole life as a series of painful failures in the face of this ridiculous death? Are the last images of life, or the first of death, the ones that drive you downward, your failures? Did the Macedonian man think of how his death failed his wife, his family, his own intentions for the New World?

I must beware this sympathy with the dead, for even as I place the bag next to them on Chicago's North Side, I feel the weight and absurdity of my own failures in the very act of carrying the dead. Images of my life in Chicago spill over me, pushing me down. I never aspired to haul the dead from their death places. I only wanted to be a writer, a Chicago writer, but now I am picking up dead bodies on the North Side of Chicago. The irony is a terrible weight. I look back at how I have struggled in this city, working every menial service job the city offers by the thousands: waiter, doorman; the thousands of bags I have carried, the train rides downtown looking for work with only five dollars in my pocket, applying for jobs so I can pay rent while I finish a story that won't get published and hear the personnel manager ask, "Where do you see yourself in five years?" I remember long days in studio apartments wondering what I was doing wrong. Here in the city where my parents were born and raised and my family began, I see them seeing me, my father's disgust at my announcement that I wanted to become a writer, that I wanted to become a police officer as a means of seeing the city as it is, as a means of giving me the time and money to write on my own. I look at myself in a basement opening a body bag, and perceive the disconnection of my life from my most intense passions, and I can feel a weight descend upon me and spill over me.

I sit in the wagon after we have loaded a body in the back.

"Poor ol' Jerome Williams," my partner Brian says as he enters the wagon, referring to today's dead man we have just loaded. He died in a government-paid apartment, clearly a longtime welfare recipient. "He ain't going to work today."

I smile.

"Yes. Perhaps it was all the overtime that did him in," I respond, and we both chuckle.

I must be honest. Not all the dead descend.

Several weeks earlier, my partner and I picked up a two-month-old baby, who had died under suspicious circumstances. We were called to a hospital in Evanston, an affluent suburb next to Chicago's North Side. The mother and father claimed they had looked in on him at 5 a.m. and he was fine. By 9 a.m. the parents said they found him dead. The doctor said he had been dead longer than that; the rigor mortis and lividity—the first time I even heard that word—indicated he had died several hours earlier. The death was ultimately ruled sudden infant death syndrome, as the boy, who was next to his twin brother in bed, lay facedown. But when we found him in the hospital, he was on his back, his legs and arms falling easily at his side, seemingly open either to death or life, regretting or fighting neither. He seemed peacefully dead. The nurse carried the infant to the wagon wrapped in small sheets and a blanket, sensing correctly and compassionately that neither my partner nor I could touch him yet. By the way she carried him, his lightness was palpable. There was no heaviness. He rode in the front seat of the wagon between my partner and me, too small to be placed in a body bag in the back of the wagon. Both of us were careful not to touch him and desperate to arrive at the morgue. Both of us were silent, fighting back tears and thinking about a forgiving God, our own children, or the children we might have had.

That child, and a senior in a nursing home suffering from dementia, did not seem burdened in their final position. Otherwise, I believe the dead are of the same mind.

Our regular intrusions into the world of the dead provide wagon men with more knowledge than is good for them. In addition to hauling the dead, we often mull over the case reports that provide crucial points of information in their descent. We read them and talk about them on the way to the morgue, as well as any other information gleaned from witnesses and officers familiar with the case. We often linger for hours at a death scene, waiting for the investigation to conclude. We have learned the narrative structure of the dead. The theme is ostensibly the cause of death, listed on the certificate, but wagon men learn the dead weight begins in the living, far earlier than official declarations. We can spot those more likely to be dead soon. Most are simple enough: a drug addict, a terminally ill man talking suicide. But in time I can see the weight in victims, offenders, and witnesses as we respond to calls like domestics, batteries, and burglaries. As the people talk, we see the dead weight oozing out of their delusions, their depressions, their cruelty, their fears, their apathy, and, yes, even their love. Wagon men, even more than other police officers, feel the weight. Sometimes in the course of our work, we must touch them, either to move them out of the way, to get their attention, or to arrest them, and there it is, an unnatural slowness, a weight.

It has begun.

Many newly arrested, for example, are upbeat when we take them toward the wagon, joking and lighthearted with their handcuffs on as we walk across the parking lot to the waiting wagon, my partner in front and me in the rear. They smile and joke as we sit them on the metal seat and pull the safety bar across their midsection and lock it, saying "just like the amusement park" to make light of their incarceration and prolong their good mood. But when we open the wagon door in the garage of the lockup twenty minutes later, they are silent, sullen, and they have sunk far down, their head resting on the safety bar or their body slumped all the way into the corner where we place the dead. They emerge angry and disgusted in the enclosed garage of the lockup, the reality of the humiliating process ahead of them setting in, often coupled with the fact that it was a loved one who called the police and signed a complaint against them. This is the beginning of a descent. There will be more arrests, more sunken rides in the wagon, possibly drugs, and then we or some of our wagon brothers will arrive to place them in a body bag after death comes in one form or another, suicide, murder, or car wreck.

"When will I get out?" they always ask us as we walk into the lockup.

"You feel that weight? You must get rid of that," I want to tell them.

"In about four hours," I say.

How complex and ominous the weight is. How distant its origins. I think about the descent of the Macedonian man. Did it begin in Europe? From the high hopes during the flight over, to the sixth floor when he took the elevator to the lobby, then down the stairs to the laundry room, where he met his murderer(s)? What thoughts preoccupied him that he didn't see it coming, that he couldn't escape, or that he was foolish enough to fight? Did he cry out? The exodus from his homeland to an apartment in Chicago, perhaps explained as a move upward in the world, but in reality distancing him from what he knew and loved, isolated.

I walked three floors of apartments above him, asking each resident if they heard anything unusual below them.

"Why?" they asked, surprised by the police so early in the morning.

"There was a death," I said, and they stare at me silently.

The weight. When was the first sip of alcohol? When was the first sense that life is too heavy? When was the first move toward crime, the slinking into back doors? When did the bar become such a cozy, inviting solitude?

I think of the Russian man we found on the floor next to the couch in the basement who had a bottle of vodka on the coffee table, along with his wallet and keys. He lived in an apartment upstairs, but for reasons we never heard he built this little hideaway in the basement. A former boxer in his homeland, he drank too much and apparently fell, striking his head against the table, struggled for a while, then died on the floor. He wasn't found for two days. The back of his head oozed out the mixture of secretions we have grown to expect from the dead. A large, muscular man, we struggled to get him out of the cramped basement, down a long walkway, and into the wagon waiting in an alley. Several times we had to stop and set him down on the concrete sidewalk. The sound of a dead body on the sidewalk is unique, soft decaying flesh on unforgiving concrete. It causes us to tighten up when we hear it. While stopped, we breathed heavily for a while until we could carry him again, our breath coming out in a fog in the cold weather, counting one, two, three, before we lifted again, our backs straining against the awkward, uncooperative weight. A few neighbors arriving home through the alley caught a glimpse of us lifting the black body bag into the wagon and gaped. I felt disrespectful to move him. Nothing could articulate his life more than that scene in the basement. There was nothing else he wanted to say.

You see how the dead drag the living with them? When we told the wife of the Macedonian man that her husband, whom she had seen only a little while earlier, was dead by foul play—a phrase she needed explained by a relative standing next to her—she immediately sank to the ground, unable to stand anymore. There she cried softly, then she and the rest of the relatives sat in the lobby of the apartment building slumped over the chairs and couches, their heads hung down, tears falling, and often shaking their heads. This is the position they will assume for the months to come, the widow sitting sullen in their apartment.

I look at myself again in the passenger seat of the wagon. I inspect my hands and the sleeves of my shirt for any remnants of the dead for the fifth of sixth time. I still feel the soft, mushy touch of the dead man we just hauled to the morgue. I glance at the bottoms of my boots for any secretions that might contaminate the wagon. Nothing. I have become skilled in handling the dead efficiently and without mistakes. I have learned to deal with the morgue attendants, who try to shuffle their paperwork off on us and get us to haul the bodies into their examining rooms. I look over at my partner, who remains untroubled by the dead, whereas I am slumped down in my seat, reading the case report again. I cannot shrug off the dead as my partner does. Why?

Suddenly the logic of hauling the dead overwhelms me, for the one terrifying truth a wagon man learns early on is that the weight is not arbitrarily imposed upon a life, it arises from somewhere deep within ourselves. The world, a wagon man learns, is not in its essence mechanical. It is moral and fateful, and I wonder what it means that I now haul the dead in the neighborhood where my parents were born, my family began, and I settled after fifteen years in Chicago. As I pore over the case reports of the deceased and pass the buildings where I have removed them, pondering the details of their demise that stayed in my imagination, I feel as if the dead have brought out something in me. I have, in their silent presence, confronted my own weight: reading their narratives, I have read my own. Seeing their weight, I have seen mine.

Are the dead, I wonder, teaching me or ruining me?

My partner's mood lightens up after we leave the morgue. It is too late in the day now to be assigned another removal. Any death scenes will now wait for the next watch in a few hours.

"What the hell?" my partner will say of any new removals. "They ain't going nowhere."

Both of us are also heartened by the fact that, according to the new union contract, the police will no longer haul dead bodies in a few more weeks. I feel such gratitude to the union, for despite my dark ruminations, I realize now as we distance ourselves from our last run how much I hate removing the dead. I am tired of their clumsy, filthy death places. I am tired of their stench and their silence, and tired of the unbridgeable gulf between us. I am tired of pulling the dead into the living, no matter what insight they might provide, no matter what secrets they may reveal.

We drive awhile longer. I sense my partner wants to push the issue of lunch again, the only constant power struggle between us. It is already an hour past our regular meal time and enough time has lapsed to displace the aura of the morgue. I sense him squirming in his seat, preparing to suggest one of his favorite fast-food restaurants. I sit and wait, my mind already made up.

"How 'bout a sausage pizza today over on Western Avenue, Mr. Marty?" he finally asks diplomatically.

I pause a moment, looking out my window, then smile.

"Pizza sounds good to me," I say, my spirits finally lifting.

THE
CHORUS

As we turn the wagon around in response to the call on the radio, it dawns on me that I returned to Chicago to bear the dead. I do not bear them only as a burden, though I dread the scene we are about to enter, but because they must be carried, must be listened to. Their song begins now as we drive up the alley, the bright autumnal leaves thrashing against the wagon, the morning light shining through them as if announcing an epiphany. The dispatcher told us to meet the detectives in the rear, meaning the alley, but nothing more. The alley is so lush we must drive slowly, anxious about the scene. We exit the wagon and stand next to it, the engine running. There is a pile of smoldering debris, and the smell of burning roof tiles and old wood is strong. A few detectives and evidence technicians are standing quietly, apologetic in their manner for the task they have imposed on us. There is the burnt car where the garage once stood, and then we see it, a large clump of brown-and-black mass with some smoldering clothes on it, the torso of a burned man. We look at each other, put on our gloves, and grab the body bag. We lift and place the torso in it easily, struck by its lightness, then rummage through the debris for an arm, a leg, a hand, and put them in the bag.

The chorus no longer catches us off guard as it once did. We do not walk into its song vulnerable and distracted, the intensity of the scenes mixing with the tenets of the song. We move slowly into it, beginning with the foreboding voice on the radio: a removal, check the well-being, concerned neighbor, gunshots. We have developed our own rituals and attitudes to stave off the chorus, then face it slowly as the detectives reveal the facts of the demise and we prepare for the task ahead of us.

"Can I give you a hand?" I ask my partner, holding up the burnt one I have just found under some tiles, then tossing it in the bag.

This victim was a newspaper delivery man. He lies next to his beat-up old car. Half-burnt newspapers blow all around the scene. We surmise the job as a deliveryman was only to fund his drug habit and that was what led him to this block where drugs are sold steadily. Few people have a paper delivered in the neighborhood. Somehow he was led to the alley and into the garage, the raging sound of the flames alerting the neighbors who were just getting up.

We gather these details from the detectives, who guess accurately that the fire was not the cause of death. The medical examiner will later confirm it, discovering the bullet in the back of his head during the autopsy. The victim is known to the detectives, a career addict always in debt to someone. He must have been duped to come to the spot, for there are no signs he was forced into the garage, they say. One detective holds a copy of the victim's mug shots and rap sheet, several pages long. But we only half hear the facts they gather as we are flooded by the favored themes of the chorus: the irony, the delusion, the cruelty. They dance about the scene in the colors of the morning.

I spot people looking out their second-story windows at us, confirming in their glimpses of the body bag the rumors that someone had indeed been murdered in their alley. Our eyes meet for a moment when we look up at them. Our humor fades as well. We work silently.

I recall how the ancients acknowledged the power of the chorus, affording it the primary role in their tragedies. They suspended movement of the play, giving the stage over to it, as movement and time seem suspended when the chorus rises in the city, in scenes such as this one.

It is demise that most invokes the chorus, rising up with a power and presence such that it appears to thrum broodingly in this world and with certainty in the next, as if in some way it is a bridge or vessel bearing us between the two. Holding presence in both worlds, there is a presumption of epiphany in its song. At least I conceive that there is, for I believe that, like the ancient city, the dead are carried by its citizens, that their chorus resonates and can be heard. I believe, for example, this man heard the flames dancing around his body even after he was shot, flames being, for him, the appropriate song for his stupid, wasted, cruel life, and the sound that remains with him even now as we dig through the smoldering remains.

"Bring out your dead," I often shout out the window of our wagon when we are lumbering down a narrow street, making light of what we have become, knowing any minute the radio may call our beat and send us to another removal.

"What is his name?" the hostile morgue attendant asks, referring to the corpse in the wagon.

"Hold on," I say. I return a few moments later and shrug my shoulders. "He won't say." She then smacks the paperwork down on the counter and walks away.

Each day we discuss our latest plan. My partner and I notice the mannequins at a store going out of business, working on our plan steadily. We will buy one and dress it up in some clothes. We will put it in a body bag but leave it partially unzipped so that part of the head and arm stick out. We will leave it in the wagon after we check off for the day, waiting for the next watch to drive away with it in the back, wondering under what circumstances they will finally open the back door and see it. We work out this joke daily, adding details and covering all angles, the image of the two cops discovering it in the back sending us into fits of laughter. What will they do? Who will they call?

The chorus is communal, invoking a similar state of mind to all those within earshot, the way the sacred sometimes can. How fortunate, how civilized that the ancients should let the chorus have full voice in their plays, that the chorus should be absorbed into their highest art and religion. Not for us in Chicago. The chorus is not yet sanctioned. Instead, it lingers in the unofficial places of the unadorned city, places where the dead and dying go, places where the desperate linger, like this alley. All morning the residents will gaze out their windows, linger in their backyards to get a closer look, whisper the details among each other. All morning the cops will come, pulling into the alley, waiting for the right moment to approach the officers on scene and gather the details. Veteran cops gently send away the gazers when they gather too closely, knowing their approach is irresistible.

My own voice joins the chorus. It is the sound of my arguments five years earlier in favor of becoming a police officer. The job, I had told myself then, would be a step up in life. Now, standing in the center of this man's lethal delusions, I see myself in my forties, bent over his charred torso, picking up his hand and placing it in the bag (I never knew hands were so heavy). I hear my voice arguing that joining the police will be a move toward a career, away from the menial jobs that have comprised my life in other uniforms: doorman, waiter, bartender; there have been so many. The chorus begins laughing now in the quiet of the alley. I see myself as it sees me, this the most degrading job I have ever undertaken. It is worse than any of the jobs I have endured in the city, the dishes I have washed, the bags I have carried, the job interviews I have lied my way through. It raises the sound of my deluded arguments for becoming a cop, as if this dead man and the manner of his death echo the delusions of my own reasoning and the hubris of my imagined ascendancy. In the moments our delusions become clear, the chorus rises in vindictive voice, as it must have risen in the mind of this man we are placing in the bag, the foolishness of his intent that led him to the alley, the self-destruction of his drugs finally clear, the flames rising around him. Our greatest delusions, the ones that give us the most confidence, these are the targets of the chorus, called hubris by the ancients.

That I should now be hauling this man and so many others in my parents' city makes perfect sense. It is why I returned to the city more than a decade ago, why so much of my life in Chicago lingers in the unadorned city: employee entrances at the rear of large buildings, basements where the workers gather and eat in sterile cafeterias, late-night train rides home looking over my shoulder as I purchase a ticket, alleys and basements removing the dead. These bottom places seem to me starting points, essential places where the chorus lingers, including the dead and their death scenes. My immersion in them signifies my increasing intimacy with the chorus, and provides some context to the otherwise incoherent movement of my life. I look around at others oppressed in some labor, ascending some career as I once tried, and I realize that, more than ever, my labor reflects my imagination. I cannot deny it, and as I look outside as we exit the alley in the wagon, heading for the morgue, I am grateful that I do not have to explain this latest conclusion: I have pursued the chorus because it is real, more real than anything in the city.

The chorus emerged in my life through uniforms, beginning with the heavy doorman uniform I was given on my first day at the

Allerton Hotel. It was too tight, and I found myself squeezing my shoulders together in an attempt to force the sleeves down on my arms. I wore a policeman's hat, white shirt, tie, and black shoes. The sounds of horns, trucks, a car radio, and a policeman's whistle hit me when I walked out the hotel door onto the street, along with the bright colors of taxis. I eyed the skyline of the city, the immense buildings lining Michigan Avenue. I stood awkward and anxious.

I was out of money and I needed this job badly. I had been trained for three days by the regular doorman, Willie, whose stutter and southern black accent were so pronounced I rarely understood what he meant. I nodded when he spoke, said "excuse me" several times, then pretended as if I understood him. Each of the three days Willie trained me, he gave me ten dollars, enough to get home, buy coffee and something to eat in the morning, then get back to work the next evening. I gathered from watching Willie the three previous days that I was to make money helping guests with their luggage, as well as parking the cars of certain people who wanted to go shopping or eat across the street. Others were to be rejected. Technically, parking cars in front of the hotel was illegal, but I learned from Willie that every doorman parked a few cars and the police rarely interfered. Willie had a whole system of evaluating a potential parker that I never understood, but it was a good system because every car he parked resulted in ten dollars when the owner returned. I eyed his wad of bills with envy as he added a fresh ten to it. I had been broke ever since I returned to the city. Initial attempts at career jobs eroded into finding a way to pay rent. I felt my desperation keenly, compounded by the fact that I was a recent college graduate.

There were certain strict rules I did understand, repeated gravely by Willie and the front desk manager: Never block traffic on the street, keep the front of the hotel clear, and never park a car on the other side of the street, where numerous signs warned of immediate towing.

My first day without Willie, within two hours I had done all three. From the flow of traffic along Huron Street, cars would suddenly veer to the right in front of me, drivers and passengers jumping out, trunks popping open. The passengers would begin barking questions about parking and restaurants, then said they would move the car after they checked in. On the street level beneath so many skyscrapers, I still could not determine north and south. The guests would disappear into the hotel. Many did not return for several hours, the car sitting in front. What was I going to do, I asked myself, have a guest's car ticketed or towed my first day on the job?

I lacked the calm, knowledgeable persona I had observed in so many other doormen, including Willie, an assumed quality of all Michigan Avenue doormen. "It's a tough job, running the door. I hope you can handle it," the general manager had said to me. I rushed from car to car, trying to get the keys to the cars before the guests went inside the hotel. After one hour the front door was completely blocked and I had cars piled all the way back to the alley, no spot available for anyone to check in. The arriving guests were forced to double-park in front of me, causing a backup of rush-hour traffic behind them, horns blaring my incompetence. All four luggage carts were stuffed with suitcases and hanging bags. I never had time to push them inside, and I had already forgotten who they belonged to. From Willie I had observed the importance of keeping the keys in some kind of order, so that when the driver returned you quickly found them and opened the car door, but now there was a mass of them in my coat pocket, a kind of metal Gordian knot I had to separate each time I wanted to move a car. Most drivers were smaller than I, so getting in and out of cars in my large coat with the cap on was a great effort. I emerged clumsily with the hat off, my hair a mess and my shirt untucked. One time I left the keys in a car and searched for them frantically for five minutes before I spotted them in the ignition. People were stopping to ask me questions, and I just walked past them to move a car to an open spot.

A mass of cars jammed into the small loading area of the hotel, with me moving them as closely as I could, sometimes the back or the front end jutting incoherently into the street. I put the hazard lights on most of them, which, I admitted later, only drew more attention to the chaos I was creating on Huron Street. There was no alternative. I was blocking traffic too much: I had to put two cars across the street.

At first I did not hear the hydraulic motor, so lost was I in running from car to car. But after a while I looked up toward the sound and saw two of my parked cars, both guests of the hotel, hooked onto the blue city tow trucks that had the ominous sign STREETS AND SANITATION on the side. The motor pulled the cars closer to the truck, as if desiring them. The tow truck drivers were directed angrily by a beat cop.

My dreams of a steak dinner after work, and possibly even a cab ride home, faded into the image of begging for my job, which is where I was ten minutes later, sitting in the office of the hotel manager, who wanted me gone.

It had been a long demise, longer than the first few days of working at the hotel before this hotel job. There had been washing dishes in a café, busboy for a catering company, and the final descent the day before the hotel job, as a bouncer on Rush Street, the center of nightlife for the college aged in the city. The bouncer job meant standing outside at the entrance, where a long line of drunk, screaming kids waited in the cold as I checked their IDs. I eyed each license as it was flashed in front of me, not even bothering to do the math for the cutoff dates, not really even looking at the birthdays, hearing only the cacophony of their belligerent questions and rude demands to enter.

"What the fuck, man? It's cold out here."

The women wore revealing clothes, stared at me with faces covered in stylish makeup. They hurled curses and demands in slurred speech. The other bouncers had learned to laugh and play along with their rudeness, trying to connect with the patrons, but I remained sullen. The bouncers enjoyed the perks of the job, like free drinks and bedding an inebriated patron or waitress by the end of the night. I was caught by the manager allowing several people with fake IDs in, and my apathy during the scolding was observed. I just nodded and went back to the front door.

"Get your fucking hands off me," I wanted to say to the next patron who took the liberty of patting me on the back, but I only glared without smiling, looking past the line of drunks down the street to the L station. That's where I was standing when the head bouncer, a onetime semipro football player, told me it was time to put on the costume.

"What are you talking about?"

"You have to wear the costume. We all take turns," he said.

"What costume? No one told me anything about a costume."

"Yeah. It's in the back, and you are up in about an hour."

I walked to a back room, and there hanging from a water pipe was the costume of a huge dog, complete with a dog head that fit over my own. There were no turns. The dog detail was just their way of getting rid of me by making me go first, a test of whether someone had the requisite subservience for a bouncer. I was furious at the deception. The head bouncer told me I had to wear the costume on the dance floor, dancing wildly with the drunken yuppies, who, I imagined, would paw and push me, maybe even pour their drinks on me; the uniform smelled of stale beer. I was supposed to keep dancing jubilantly in their abuse. It was quiet in the room, far away from the noise of the bar. I contrasted the stupid grin of the dog with my misery, imagined walking from the quiet of this back room into the noise of the next wearing the costume. Without formally making up my mind, I began walking slowly toward the front of the bar, out the door, and toward the L tracks, aware of the gaze of the other bouncers and that I had not even worked long enough to collect some tips.

Educated man, the chorus laughed. *Bright future*. How easily and brutally it reduces. How inevitably it rises from our delusions in the city. How quickly the chorus adopts the dead, for the voices that inevitably rise up in the chorus are foregone ones, voices of fathers and forefathers. They ridiculed me on the walk home, the next day, never letting me forget my return to my father's city, ridiculing me as I stopped to make certain I had enough money for the train ride home and realized I did not.

And here again the chorus employs the dead, for this dead man we are bagging now seems suddenly its willful agent. We are suspicious of him. Once gone, the dead labor for the chorus. It is all he can do not to cackle wildly in the bag at the ruminations he initiates. He cannot wait to get into the back of the wagon, where he can relax and relive the song he has imposed on me. He effuses as much stench and weight as the chorus will allow, and at the morgue he and the other dead poke each other in their mirth and whisper the stories of their death scenes when no one living can hear. To imagine the police department as a means of ascendancy when the city has always led me to the chorus is a delusion he and all the other dead relish. *Bring out your dead*, they cackle, the same cackling this victim heard when the flames rose up around his incapacitated body, cursing the crazy intent that led him there.

It is not reverence that makes us maintain our decorum around the dead. It is our fear of their power, their troubling alliance with the chorus, so we bear him, and all his kind, carefully. After the humiliation of the chorus, there is epiphany. Rid of our delusions, we see clearer than before, however painful. One wonders at the clarity with which the dead, so much deeper into the chorus, now see us.

I once believed, as the deluded do, that my imagination was mine, a garden of my own creation and something I controlled, but the chorus shows otherwise. The imagination comes up through roots in the darker corners of the unadorned city, pulling me along by the forces of the foregone: ancestors, the dead, institutions. The law. Bearing the dead shows I imagine little: Chicago, with its chorus, imagines me, and I have surrendered to it. That I perceive all the dead surrendering in their chorus, as a culmination of the circumstances of their life, fills me with an ominous foreboding, and a need to understand it more deeply.

Is this what the ancients meant by self-knowledge? That they flocked to the plays where the chorus sang is a sign of their courage, the certainty of their self-conception, even when that chorus lingered among the horror of their greatest sins. Small wonder, then, that banishment from their city was considered their greatest punishment, worse than a condo in Miami, than dancing as a dog with the drunken yuppies.

Yet look at me in my uniform, standing somewhat slouched on one leg and listening closely. I feel as if I have sunk lower each year. I have immersed myself in the symphonies of demise, perceiving the disturbing origins of songs. Even listening to the inane chatter of the criminal, the insane, the addicted, I hear the logic of the chorus beneath it. Less and less seems my certainty. Less and less my outward piety, more inward my religious anxiety. How welcome would be certainty.

These alliances with the dead world forebode, intensifying what meaning, what symbols we draw from the city. Perceiving the chorus so powerfully in so much demise, I cannot help but wonder if it is a hint of what is to come, the first glimpses of the other world, a possibility more ominous than any tenets of faith, for it is real and I hear it every day; it has become my calling. What did this man make of the flames surrounding him in the garage, such a clear and irrefutable sign of his life gone all wrong? What imagination placed him there? Was this the beginning of his accounting?

The chorus forces us to confront not only the song of the dead, but how we bear them now and in their demise. What is our role, the chorus asks, in their anguish? Did we bear them toward their demise or away? The chorus will not tolerate our bullshit then, our simple and false claims of innocence, and after I have placed the body in the wagon and walked to the passenger door in the narrow passage between the truck and alley fence, the chorus demands a recounting of how I have borne loved ones in their falling.

The sounds of loved ones rise up, the moans of my mother in the third year of her demise. I had found her on a winter afternoon in the living room of her house in northern Michigan. She had just returned there after her cardiac arrest and emergency surgery in the suburbs of Chicago. It began several months earlier at her sister's house in the suburbs. During the crisis, I gathered her in my arms before she could fall, pulling her close to me and telling her to fight to live as her body began the first seizures. She pulled me to her, desperately seeking my help, but only muffled moans emerged, begging me to help her. But after her heart stopped, it was my cousin who pushed me aside and performed the emergency measures that brought her back, a huge gulp of air suddenly coming from her after she lay still for so long.

Now in Michigan, she was falling into my arms again, yelling in the crises of her latest unnamed malady, her face next to my ear as I placed my arms under hers and lifted. Halfway out of the chair, the pain peaked and the moaning turned into shouts. She went limp in my arms, and I had to hold her up with all my strength. I had driven to the house that morning from Chicago, the increasing panic in her voice apparent in my phone calls to her the day before.

I noticed her look of relief when I arrived, the long listing of her symptoms, my father guiltily eating lunch at the table, not even saying hello to me.

There was a pail of water and a rag next to the piano in the area where she could no longer hold her bladder as she struggled to make it to the bathroom. When she clasped on to me, I could smell her body odor; she was too ill even to wash. She sat next to bay windows where there was only a deep darkness beyond. Her children were scattered about the country, an ambulance at least an hour away. Medicines, newspapers, lists were scattered on the table next to her, signs of her failed attempts to organize her crises. I tried to imagine the last two nights, when the pain became so unbearable, the anguish of sitting in the room alone, the pitch-black night outside her window, wondering what was wrong with her, how she could get to the bathroom, wondering if she would have another heart attack. The imagery of her last few days filled me with terror, imagining her crawling to the bathroom, never making it all the way, her husband asleep in his bedroom, never staying up with her, never taking her to the hospital. Who would she call out to, for my father had locked his door and probably could not hear her. The echoes of her chattering family must have filled her mind during the night, the calls with suggestions and advice intensifying the isolation, the voices of loved ones far away who speak but do not hear.

The chorus will not let me forget, not in Chicago. I wander Rogers Park, her childhood neighborhood, removing the bodies here. I believe the chorus was instrumental in putting me here, reminding me this was the city she loved, where she always wanted to return. I had carried her so many times, carried her now to the bathroom, carried her in her cardiac arrest, carried her, I must admit it, to this house and these two nights alone. It was I who bore her away from the good care she received in the city. It was I who gave in to my father and let her return up north, and I hear her anguish again sent directly into my ears as she leaned against me, clinging to me, holding her up as I helped her to the bathroom. The chorus reminds me: I knew she would end up this way. I knew it, and it was I who bore her to this chair. I send a silent missive to her every day, a missive that can only be called a prayer: Forgive me, Mom. Please, please forgive me.

The ancients warned never to measure a life until it was over, a time when the chorus has sole authority. Then its song arises with a disturbing authenticity, unifying things that once seemed distinct, antagonistic, like our intent and our fortune. Its fatefulness is rich in its attendant motifs of tragedy, metaphor, allegory, comedy, and irony. How well it illuminates life, and how impossible it is to reject it once it emerges.

What solidarity the chorus formed among the ancients as they left the plays, how much stronger their bonds of citizenship, how repulsive and vulgar became the cacophonic chatter of the deaf and the deluded outside the theater. How numerous are the tokens of flight and denial, the monuments to the dizzy dreams of happiness, fulfillment, and perfect health of the deaf and deluded. How easily are our accounts or viewpoints dismissed in their hubris, those filled with the drunken confidence of power in the city, of those who call themselves educated, who have climbed with certainty the worldly rungs of success.

Barbaric city. How much better did the ancients hear.

We place the book in the empty interview room, on the table so it will catch the eye of any officer who walks by. We place it so they can easily read the cover: 1001 *Pornographic Pictures*. Inside there is a battery and wire, the oldest and most reliable practical joke ever invented. We mill around the desk, waiting for the next victim, pretending we are working intently. It doesn't take long. The officer, in plainclothes, spots the book and walks over. He picks it up, reads the title. The suspense kills us. He squints, wondering if it was obtained from an offender and accidentally left there. He looks out the door to see if anyone is watching, looks left and right, turns around with his back to us, pulls the book closer, and opens it.

"Motherfucker!" he shouts as the current zaps his hands, the book dropping to the floor with a loud bang. The entire front desk, some ten officers, break up.

"You fucking assholes," he says, but then smiles. He is the fifth or sixth victim of the morning. Within a few minutes he resets it and joins us, waiting for the next one.

We walk outside, turning up our radios slightly, listening.

STUDIO
APARTMENTS

There was only the steady sound of my breath and my footsteps, interrupted every few minutes by the sound of an approaching car. I slowly turned to face it as I emerged at the end of the ramp, my hand outstretched and my thumb pointed down the interstate. I would make eye contact with the driver, hoping to communicate in that moment that I was nothing more than a student looking for a ride. (Almost always my rides would say, "I usually don't pick up hitchhikers, but you looked like an all-right guy.") I was on my favorite ramp, the Westnedge exit of Interstate 94 in Kalamazoo, Michigan. When there were no cars, I turned around and walked along the shoulder, and as I walked, I occasionally lifted my eyes and glanced down the interstate. There were two other ramps in view, each about a half mile apart, populated with a gas station advertising snacks and hot coffee and filled with idling trucks taking respite from the bitter cold winter weather, a small cloud of black exhaust flowing out the top.

It was still early morning on a weekday, and I should have been in class. I was only a few months out of high school, but already for me college had lost its promise. I attended only literature classes and read only books that excited me, then read more of them in the library, regardless of whether they were on the syllabus. Straight A's at first, now I was flirting with flunking out altogether. Each day I woke up early in the morning, left my rented room, and walked to class, then headed for the library. It was a time in the Midwest when all the cities reeled from the decline of the automobile industry and, even for a student, jobs were scarce. Kalamazoo was a miserable town, composed of various neighborhoods called ghettos: the student ghetto, the black ghetto, the Latin ghetto. Broken-down houses littered the landscape, with smoke coming out decrepit chimneys and dogs barking from fenced-in yards. Battered cars lined the streets. Like almost all midwestern cities, the downtown was empty, the buildings abandoned.

Aside from literature, nothing stimulated me more than the short trips I took by hitchhiking around Michigan, to Lansing to see my sister who lived on a farm, to Detroit to visit my parents. I hitchhiked Interstate 94 the most, on sections between Kalamazoo and Detroit, and on the smaller roads that fed into the interstate. The traffic on this interstate was slow and steady, more like a country road than an interstate. Country roads were preferable because cops rarely stopped me, and I obtained many pleasant rides from local people coming and going from work. I stood for hours on roads next to farms, forests, under bridges when the rains were heavy, waiting out the storm, feeling the bridge shake when a large truck rolled through. I met salesmen, prison guards, preachers, autoworkers, students, drug dealers. I liked the fatigue after a long trip, the feeling that I had made it, and I didn't mind walking for hours.

Because of the cold, there was little traffic, and I was the only pedestrian on the horizon. Drivers could take a long look at me as they approached, then had plenty of room to stop. After they passed, I could turn and walk awhile longer, then turn around again when I heard another car.

I had never been to Chicago as an adult. My family had moved to the northern suburbs of the city, then to the suburbs of Detroit when I was a child. I knew little about the city except what my parents had told me about growing up on the Far North Side, in a neighborhood called Rogers Park, during the Depression and then the war. A woman I knew from Michigan, Gloria, had recently moved there to attend Loyola University. Even better, she called herself a poet and had turned me on to some of my first writers. She liked cafés and T. S. Eliot and Ezra Pound, and I found I did, too. "Why don't you come visit," she asked me at a party in Kalamazoo. *Why don't I*, I thought, the prospect of traveling to a large city where my family began stirring me. So I woke up early on a Friday morning, put on extra socks, boots, and my winter coat.

One ride was a guy fresh out of the military. He had a sports car and a large sum of money. He was traveling around the country for several months until he settled down. We rode the first stretch of the trip west on I-94, moving slowly in the cold weather through small towns and forests. Another was a tradesman, who took me the final leg of the trip in a battered pickup laden with his tools in the back. We listened to the news on his old AM radio, talking very little. I stared out the window at the forests in Michigan as we rode. He told me he was taking the toll road, stopping just south of Chicago. Normally, hitchhikers avoid toll roads because the police will almost certainly arrest you there, but I said nothing.

The city was immense and silent on the lake in the bitter cold when I rounded the toll road in Indiana and was dropped off with the first view of it. I stood on the shoulder eyeing Chicago, bathed in a blue light, crisp and clear from the sky and the lake. I spotted a train station up ahead in the middle of the toll road. I hopped the fence and was told by a guy in the ticket booth that, yes, it did lead to the city. The train approached along the lake on the south side, first through industrial areas, then working-class neighborhoods, row after row of brick and stone two-flats, dropping me downtown in the middle of the sprawling high-rises and crowded streets, yellow and red cabs prowling the downtown.

The colors and movement on the street pleased me so much then that I never stopped swimming in it. I became a doorman for more than a decade, walking the front of the hotel, then became a cop, wandering my beat.

I found the elevated train to the North Side, the red-brick buildings flying past me after we emerged from the downtown tunnel, the names of the streets called out by the conductor familiar from the stories my parents told of growing up on the North Side: Fullerton, Sheridan, Thorndale, Granville, then finally Loyola, the university my father attended after the war. From the Loyola L stop, I walked the last few blocks to Gloria's apartment, Lake Michigan in view at the east end of all the streets.

Chicago seemed to arise from the melancholy of the Midwest, an aching, immense power. It shook off the doldrums of Michigan, would not accept them. It made me restless, hungry for more, curious. Gloria stayed in a vintage building turned into student apartments. She balanced the city with literature, letting me attend classes with her after days of rambling the neighborhoods. When she was gone, I walked streets where my parents grew up.

Every week for the next six months, I would walk to Interstate 94 on the same ramp and make my way to Chicago with the same ease, staying for a weekend, a week, reading intensely, wandering, my mind on fire, all of the city's colors, movements, faces poignant.

We have placed the dead woman in the police wagon. The other police officers and I stand on the sidewalk peeling off our gloves and breathing heavily, sweat dripping down our faces, muttering soft curses that would offend no one.

"Damn, that was a hard one," one cops says.

"Never thought we could get her out of that bathroom."

The woman, in her forties, somewhat heavy with dark hair, died in the bathtub, rolling into it in the spasms of a cardiac arrest that began during defecation. The shower curtain and rod were pulled down on top of her, indicating a struggle to pull herself up, to keep fighting. She was not found for several days. The bathroom was small, off the corner of a hallway. She was stiff and filthy, having rolled in her own feces. It took more than a half hour to pull her out of the tub and onto the floor in the hallway where we could get a bag around her, the pulling and lifting causing a tear in my gloves and the first instance of me touching a dead body directly. We tried different angles, different ways of carrying her and forcing the body out of the little room. It was hard to lean over the bathtub and get any leverage on her heavy body. Eventually, we had to step into the tub. It was hot in the bathroom, with no window or ventilation, and our shirts were wet. Most of us took off our vests and set them in the squad cars because of the heat, our brows dripping as we fought to get her into the bag, up the steep stairs, and into the truck.

Whenever we linger at a death scene, something true is always left behind by the dead, something which inevitably compels those of us who enter the death scene, with no previous knowledge of the deceased, to measure the life that was and the cause of its termination. A thread unravels, a thread that connects the life and the death in a puzzling and frustrating manner, for, as public servants, we are obliged to describe the scene in the language and pretensions of the law, by the requirements of our profession and the empiricism of the living. But it is a requirement that does not suffice. What is more powerful, more accurate is our collective response, the meaning that comes to us in intangible ways and illuminates what may seem inconsequential. The dead, for their part, leave little that could be called evidence in the living world beyond the altar of their death. It does not diminish their impact; it increases it. The themes we perceive at these death scenes come to us in the most unpredictable ways and with a desperate intention, as if the dying have willfully imparted them to us. And these themes, having their origins in two worlds, draw no easy conclusions, arguing at the same time for both the theme of life, its deepest meaning, as well as the cause of its death.

Our responses to these scenes are often beyond the scope of public service. Inevitably we turn inward, imposing and measuring the same theme upon our lives, stirring old, buried memories and desires. Now my employment, this death scene, has stirred an ancient memory of my first trip to Chicago from my freshman year of college.

"Look at all these collection letters," one cop says when we begin investigating the apartment, handing them around the room, the quiet of the apartment interrupted only by the occasional chatter of our radios. We imagine the letters coming in the mail every day. Someone else points silently to the dozens of pill boxes bearing ominous names with Latin origins, each one a signpost of her demise. Some of the medications deal with the physical, some the mental, the most recent ones deal only with pain. We survey the room as one officer assembles the requisite information for the case report, a process that can take a few hours. Until it is completed, we will not remove her from the bathroom. We only linger.

The chorus of her demise litters her apartment: statements from her employer about the status of her disability insurance, bills from collection agencies. It is a studio apartment, down a short flight of stairs in a small complex. Everything is organized meticulously, the medicines above the refrigerator, collection letters, the disability notices. The contrast of this organization with the encroaching filth of her apartment indicates a losing battle, as if she abdicated the larger, unmanageable tasks of cleaning an entire room in favor of organizing smaller, manageable tasks like the paperwork and medicines. The artifacts were weighed among the statements of the landlord. They reveal a family torn apart, her children and siblings no longer in contact with her. Her battle in the apartment, which had, according to the landlord, lasted years, was obviously a solitary one.

Her walls are filled with quotes from the New Testament, reminders of the power of God and prayer, of ultimate forgiveness and peace. The landlord, a kind man, had worked with her after she quit her job, lowering the rent, then forgetting about it altogether the last few months, providing more intimate details on her relationship with her family, her maladies. She suffered from heart disease and leukemia. The landlord liked her and cared for her, and her death troubles him.

She elicits the same response from us. We feel as if this apartment has been transformed into an altar as the fading autumn sun illuminates it. The filth and degradation of her body in the bathroom appears heroic from her struggle to rise up. A gentleness, a humanity, and a sincerity linger in the apartment in the quotes of the New Testament on the wall, statements about endurance, faith, and love, the kind of conviction that exudes and sustains a deep humanity. There is none of the judgment, spitefulness, or condemnation of the Old Testament, nothing in the apartment that is left to condemn the estranged family, no bitterness at a life ended too early, no rage at the cruelty of the employer or the coldness of the disability insurers, or the failures of the medical people to save her. In the things present and the things absent, the elements of a living religion linger around the body: endurance, faith, forgiveness, purity of heart.

The other cops and I have already drawn conclusions. I believe that if her family members had returned at any stage of her demise, they would have been forgiven. I believe without ever having known this woman that they abandoned her. Her entire family has moved away from Chicago. The landlord has called the brother in another state, and within moments he is asking about her TV.

I recall the many times I lost my temper when caring for my

mother, traveling five hours to northern Michigan from Chicago after working late the night before, my nerves frazzled. I would walk into the house, and my mother, suffering in various degrees of dementia, would pour out questions on insignificant subjects, so lonely was she to talk to someone. Too often I was unable to bear them and cut her off, often in a burst of temper. I think of the difference it made in my life that I knew before I even asked a few minutes later that I was forgiven.

After we have placed her in the wagon, I see the other officers milling outside the building and in the stairwell outside the apartment, lost in reveries. None of them are gathered in groups talking about investments, the injustices of the job, or politics, the way cops normally do. Each officer lingers quietly, waiting for a supervisor to announce the end of the investigation, to release this death scene back to the living.

What makes such scenes an altar, I realize, are the signs of conviction, of a private religion that endured even in the face of her impending death. It is overwhelming to enter it so quickly, without warning, and it generates images of what we find sacred in our lives. Some of the cops are thinking about loved ones, some about their deepest passions. I am thinking about the first few months in the city when I began reading literature, the origins, I would say, of my own private religion.

I walk back to the stairwell outside her studio apartment, handing the sergeant some information for the report. I take another long look inside at her life in reduction. With a bitter irony, I see her final scene had all the trappings of a devout life: the poverty, the abandonment of worldly concerns, family estrangement, loneliness. And faith. I can see how her faith carried her through the years of illness, how it helped her endure, but I can also see with terrible clarity the burden it placed on her life, the heavy cost, the constant distraction from worldly considerations, painfully obvious in her poverty. I cannot say with any certainty the value of the religious life. I cannot say with certainty the truthfulness of her convictions. There is her endurance and faith, and there is her life in this studio apartment.

The possibility and ecstasy I felt in the first few months of traveling to Chicago pushed me farther, into wider, longer trips around the country. Despite the dangers, the loneliness, I wandered, encouraged, like so many students at English departments, by the beatnik writers.

I was stranded on Interstate 5 near Sacramento when a cop stopped me, took me to an isolated exit with no traffic, and told me to hunt rides there: "Do not hitchhike on the interstate," he warned me. I knew there was a good chance I would spend that evening in the Sacramento jail. The heat beat down upon me, and I began craving water. I eyed an exit across a farm, about a mile away with more traffic, and began walking through a cornfield to get there. Halfway through the sweat poured out of me as I struggled in the thick dust, emerging desperate for water. Then I spotted a sign that said "SWIMMING, BOATING ACCESS," and a truck filled with Mexican farm laborers pulled over and I pointed to the sign and they nodded. Five minutes later we came upon a huge cold river with a general store, and I bought a quart of water and drank it down, then another. I sat in the shade, bought a large beer, and drank from that, then walked slowly into the icy river and swam for an hour as the sun began to set. I got a ride back to the highway and said to hell with the cop. A few minutes later a classic Mercedes-Benz convertible pulled over. The driver was going all the way to Canada. I rode with him for seven hours, and he dropped me at my door in Eugene, Oregon.

I traveled through the Southwest, entering northern New Mexico in the evening when an Apache picked me up in his truck, drinking beer like water from the six-pack between us and stopping every twenty miles amidst the desert to piss, becoming enraged when I, uncomfortable at our long silences in the vast desert, asked him whether his tribe had been nomadic.

"Fuck you, you white motherfucker," he exploded. "I own a farm with twenty horses. I got more money than your father, you motherfucker. I'll leave your fucking ass out here in the desert to die, you motherfucker. Is your father a fucking nomad?"

I sat quietly in fear and shame, then finally apologized. He sensed my sincerity, then began talking about his farm, his family, his horses.

I was picked up at sunset in southern Colorado by a priest who told me in a rising voice that there was no Holocaust, that the Jews were behind America's downfall.

I was picked up in Tennessee by a man in a compact car who was too drunk to drive. I sat in the backseat because he had picked up another hitchhiker, who was sleeping in exhaustion in the front seat. The driver kept looking back at me, telling me "not to fuck with" him, then he pulled out a pistol and began waving it at me, driving so recklessly that twice I had to grab the wheel from the backseat; each time I lunged forward, he moved for the pistol. He refused to let me out until we reached his turnoff, some ninety miles down the road. I kicked the side of his door three times before he could pull away, putting a large dent in it and cursing him.

A soldier picked me up in the desert of eastern Washington, telling me after riding together for a few hours that he worked in a nuclear silo and was responsible for launching nuclear weapons. He blared a rock tune as the sun went down, turning it down to tell me how they never knew during tests whether it was real or not, a strange, self-effacing smile across his face, then turned the music up again.

In west Texas in the brutal summer heat, I went two days without sleep, afraid to camp in the desert among the snakes and scorpions until I finally found a small rest area off a country road. I slept on the top of a picnic table. After a while I looked over and saw a man in a pickup truck watching me from across the road, the first vehicle I had seen in hours. I placed my knife in my hand, forcing myself to stay awake until I saw him leave.

Years later I would drive a pickup across the country for delivery in Washington, a route I had known from hitchhiking years earlier. I picked up a hitchhiker in the evening and gestured for him to ride in the back and handed him a blanket. Some one hundred miles later, I stopped for gas.

"Why," I asked, "are you going west?"

"Some people are trying to kill me," he said vacantly.

When he left for the bathroom, I set his backpack against the pump and left.

I moved out to the West Coast, not returning to Chicago for many years. When I did come back, I studied Latin in the mornings, worked as a doorman downtown at night.

William Kennedy's novel *Very Old Bones* was published five years into my life as a doorman and my fourth semester in Latin. It was late winter, a time when a doorman only scratches out a few dollars every shift. I postponed buying the novel until the semester was finished, knowing that once I started reading it, I would not concentrate on studies, but a friend handed it to me one evening as I worked the door. I stayed in my studio apartment and read it over the next three days, calling in sick at work. Then I sat at my desk, telling myself it was time to write Kennedy a letter: I had some questions. That letter took six months, the first time I thought about being a writer. I never went back to school, asking the professor for an incomplete, then never calling back.

I have always lived in studio apartments. After a while I never imagined living in anything else. I look back at all the ones I have lived in, in so many different neighborhoods, and realize how much they resemble this woman's. I wonder, with a shudder, if her death scene is a glimpse of my own.

One image the police will see on my wall is the picture of Walt Whitman's burial tomb, a grandiose tomb that shocked many people of his day. At the time of his death, Whitman lived on the second floor of the house he purchased in Camden, New Jersey, and I often think of him there ruminating on his career as he sat in his chair facing the window, his life, by many measures, built upon illusions, refusing to give up on *Leaves of Grass*, refusing to take out its most controversial sections. Once, his housekeeper, fed up at the disorder of his room, cleaned it while he was away, disturbing the piles of letters, photographs, articles, speeches, essays, and poetry, an act that sent Whitman into a rage. Whitman believed early on that his poems would lead to wealth and recognition, not to a simple room in New Jersey, living on the contributions of admirers.

I believe Whitman purchased the tomb because he feared, given the meager sales of his poems, the poor reviews, the moral indignation against their sexuality, that his poems would not last more than a generation and that some other monument would have to stand for his life, apart from his lifelong commitment to *Leaves of Grass*.

I wish a similar monument for this woman. I imagine a sepulcher and a mass in which her faith is revealed, celebrated. I banish the mumbling priest and the stale showing room of the funeral parlor, her brother perfunctorily greeting the visitors, calculating the slight worth of her few possessions as he greets them.

I stand outside the wagon, the light almost gone. I have never found the city, never found anything to point to and say "This is it," only a place where people find a way to scratch out their illusions in the images it provides. Chicago, I conclude, is not so much real as it is imagined. What freedom, what danger. We watch its residents live out lives based on what is little more than illusion, on premises we can neither prove nor dismiss. Why the city gives such freedom to illusion, such intensity to the images we choose here, I do not know.

Her death scene is moving, horrible. Her faith confronts mine. There is no such thing as certainty. The city is imagined. Perhaps, even, the living light it provides is a lie. Perhaps nothing derived from it is real and true. We see so many lives built upon, then destroyed by, delusions. Look at me. Look at this woman.

She is in the back of the wagon now. I climb into my seat after shedding the torn gloves I wore when bearing her. We begin the drive to the morgue, moving slowly and carefully and saying little to each other. I am weighted down, exalted. I feel so much sorrow for her, so much honor.

CITY
LIMITS

There is a solitude in Chicago, a solitude lucid and unwavering. This solitude comes over me as I drive westbound on Devon Avenue and a call comes on the radio. My partner, Jan, should respond, but she is on her cell phone to a new boyfriend. I keep one hand on the steering wheel and reach up to the microphone with the other, hold it closer to my ear, trying to hear it clearly amidst the buses, cars, construction, and voices along the street. There are many languages here, much shouting across the street. In the intimacy that builds between longtime partners, I take the assignment without her having to look at me. She knows I will catch it. I wait for the dispatcher, a little anxious. What? Where to now? *Caller says her boyfriend punched her and is still on scene, wants him arrested.*

Calls come more slowly in the early winter and traffic dies earlier. The cold and snow are still new; the weariness of late winter is a long way off. It is melancholy to feel the long winter ahead, but it is also peaceful after a busy summer. Jan and I have worked together long enough that we no longer need to discuss elemental tasks: who gets the radios, who drives, who writes the paper, who will talk at the domestic. Our shifts—"tours" they are called—go for hours without conversation, a sign of our intimacy and ease.

Even as we prepare the tour, we hardly speak to each other. I am settling in the squad car, adjusting the mirrors and my seat. By late afternoon when our tour begins, it is already getting dark. Jan has been talking on the phone since we left the district parking lot a few minutes ago. I always arrive early to the roll call room. Jan usually comes rushing in at the last moment because she has to pick up or drop off her son right before. She sits on the other side of the room. It's a relief when she comes in, though, as I am always afraid the commander will announce she called in sick or late and I will be forced to ride with someone else for the night.

As she talks on the phone, I realize I forgot to put my seat belt on. Jan loves when I do a routine in the car of a bumbling, easily angered older cop. As I reach around for the belt, I can't find it, so I immediately break into the routine, grasping wildly behind the seat, muttering intense curses, pretending I am having trouble keeping the car in its lane.

"Goddamn fucking belts. Jesus H. Christ Almighty," I whisper loudly. After squirming a few minutes, I pretend I am tangled, then suddenly free myself and put on the belt.

"There. That's done," I say to Jan, who is still on the phone and must suppress her laughter.

I wheel the Crown Victoria in a large loop on Devon Avenue. I just clear the curb, a satisfying move, and head eastbound to the address. I glance over at Jan. She has been on the phone for a while, a sign that this boyfriend holds great promise. I shake my head in mock disapproval. She smiles, suppresses another giggle, and turns away from me toward her window.

I prepare for the call. I read the narrative a few more times on the computer screen that sits between us. I look at the caller's name to see if it is familiar. As I do so, the solitude returns. It forces me to imagine the city as it is, driving away petty or fraudulent abstractions. I recall the address, imagine the buildings there, the residents and their apartments, the smells when we walk up the stairs. I know the history of the block, its patterns. I once marveled at veterans who always knew where they were to the exact number of the address. For years I fumbled, looking for these numbers and street signs, wondering if I would ever get it right, if I would ever know where I was. Now I am one of them. I can see the buildings and corners before I arrive. I speak calmly into the radio my exact address without looking up, even in alleys and parks. We turn the corner onto Damen Avenue, and there is the building, very much as I imagined it.

In this solitude, the most unexpected notions emerge, images that force me to pull over and jot them down, after a call, on the way up a flight of stairs, or pausing inside some apartment or in the middle of a conversation. This solitude arrives and lingers for unknown periods, either in the anticipation or recollection of these dispatches, in the silence of the car or the cacophony of disputes. Riding with strange partners, this solitude must sometimes be kept secret. Pulling over and writing causes anxiety and suspicion with strange partners, but not with Jan. With her these notes litter the car: in the visor, pockets of my jacket and vest, under the seat. The best of them I place in the fold of my wallet. They are the only ones worth the uncomfortable movements of procuring a wallet in a squad car, twisting myself to reach under the seat belt, around my gun belt, and into my pocket, then repeating the movements when I return the wallet to my pocket. But mostly these notes I scribble fall about the squad car like papers blowing around the city's abandoned factories. Who knows where they will end up?

I catch a glimpse of myself in the rearview mirror as I pull myself out of the driver's seat, seeing that in my intimacy with the city, I begin to resemble it. I am too large, spreading haphazardly out into suburbs that were once farmland. I feel my belly push against my bulletproof vest, see the beginning of my second jaw. There is salt residue on my coat from brushing up against cars. I get out of the car and lean on it. I slouch too much. I am bellicose. I have high blood pressure. I am too loud, stubborn. Like the city's worst neighborhoods, I scatter artifacts about the places I have lingered, the car littered with my rejected paperwork, ticket books.

I rise slowly from the car. I feel the tightness in my back from surgery after a melee sent me down a flight of steps a year ago. It is harder each day to unfold from the car at a call. I feel myself struggling for breath walking up three flights of stairs. On unimportant calls—noise complaints, landlord-tenant disputes—I often wait for Jan to get out of the car first. I open my door, swing my legs out, grab hold of the seat and door frame as if I am trying to pull myself out. I huff and puff, wince and moan, falling back in the seat, and then I look up at her with my arms outstretched.

"Can you help me?" I beg her.

I stare at her, exaggerating my need for breath, ignoring her laughter.

"Get the hydraulic lift machine in the trunk," I say, waving my arms frantically.

Other times I have mock attacks of incontinence in the squad car after a large meal. I stop at a red light and lean over in my seat, struggle for breath, leaning my face close to Jan's.

"God, that was a lot of chicken. Maybe too much," I say, holding my stomach. Jan shakes her head because she knows what's coming next. I stare at her, a desperate look on my face.

"Oh, Jesus God," I say, curling up into a ball, squeezing her arm tightly in terror.

I look up at her once more. "Again. Oh God. Again. Station, station. Jesus, Lord and Savior. Take me to the station."

"You fucking jackass," she says, tears welling in her eyes.

As we exit the squad car, we both notice a young male walking quickly toward us, already too close.

"Get your hands where I can see them," Jan shouts, both of us certain he is the boyfriend. He bears gang colors and walks with his hands in his coat pockets. We are leery of him. We must take control. I point to the car and he places his hands on it. I start going through his pockets, letting him ramble for a while.

"I didn't touch her . . . She owes me money . . . I just came by to get it," he babbles.

I sigh. Eighteen years old and he is demanding money from his baby's mother. The absurdity of this image does not reach him and probably never will. He lives day by day, desire by desire, moves from hunger to sex to entertainment. And now we must listen to him rail at the injustice of her claims. Part of our job is to hide our disgust; it will only escalate the tension. I go through his pockets slowly, afraid of a weapon or needle. Then I go through his belt. They often keep dope in there. I shake his pants strongly, but nothing falls to the ground.

"Sounds like you've had some tough breaks in life," I say.

"Hell yeah, I have, Officer. I'm just trying to get my life together. Man, nothing going my way, and now my girl won't give me my money," he rants, oblivious to my sarcasm.

No gun, no knife, no weed, just five condoms.

I love you, baby.

"Bitch, you owe me five bucks," I will say in the car each time we see a gangbanger walking with his girlfriend. Then I will turn to Jan. "I can't get a fucking break."

Now the girlfriend emerges onto the lawn in front of their building. Her arms are folded and she is sneering at the baby's father, whose hands are still on the hood of the squad car.

"He hit me and I want him arrested. You have to arrest him." Her statement rings false. Battery victims are rarely so demanding, so defiant. She sounds rehearsed, prepared. I shine the flashlight in her face, looking for injuries. If there are any, we must arrest him. Nothing. She takes offense at the light and gives me an ugly look and a sneer. Looks like I'll be the bad cop on this call.

I glance at Jan. Women often make fraudulent accusations against their boyfriends to get them locked up for the night. Her statements are scripted, her demands that he be locked up too considered. Most real victims let us guide them; they are so shaken up. Jan glances back at me, rolls her eyes. For a moment I imagine sitting at the station for two hours in a small room with her boyfriend handcuffed to the wall, never shutting up. I imagine trying to write the narratives on the reports with his constant chatter in our ears.

"Officer. Officer. Why would I hit my girl? She's my baby's momma."

"I don't answer rhetorical questions," I would say, knowing he doesn't know what a rhetorical question is, his confusion buying us a few moments of silence to write her fraudulent story, us completing an arrest for a trial she will never attend. A few years ago her plan might have worked. I would have concluded we had no choice but to arrest him, for she had sufficiently created all the elements of a crime: an allegation, an alleged victim, an offender, signed complaints. Even if we thought they were false, I would have blindly followed the law. *Not tonight, sweetheart.* No way. I may have been born in the day, but I wasn't born yesterday. The woman, sensing our skepticism, forces the issue.

"You'll arrest him or I'll call a supervisor," she says. Yup, she's lying. No real victim would go this route so fast.

I smile, look her in the eye, then chuckle. She doesn't like me, turns toward Jan.

"Well, tell me again what happened," Jan says.

Jan nods her head at the bullshit the woman is spinning, a gesture that encourages her to keep talking. I remain stone-faced, occasionally shaking my head. The young woman doesn't even look at me after a while. We are only barely listening, waiting for something to work with. Then it comes.

"He pushed me down, then hit me," she blurts out.

"Wait," I say, putting up my hand so that she stops talking. "What? He pushed you down?"

"Yeah. He pushed me to the ground."

"This is like a fishing story. It keeps getting bigger and bigger each time you tell it. You never said anything about being pushed down before. Let me guess. There are no bruises from that either?"

"Yeah, you never mentioned that before," Jan joins in. "I have to tell you that's very unusual."

"I'm not making this up," the woman says, but there is hesitation in her voice.

"She's fucking lying, Officer. I never pushed nobody," the boyfriend yells from the car. I put up my hand, tell him to shut up, and turn my back to him.

"Let me tell you something. You have to think out your lies better than this."

Then I pause a moment, change tones. "You don't have any witnesses, do you?"

She says nothing.

"Why don't we go upstairs and talk to everyone in your apartment and talk to some neighbors and see if anyone saw or heard anything that sounded remotely like a domestic battery? Oh, one more thing I should tell you. If you are arrested for filing a false police report, the Department of Family Services takes the kid, right?"

"No."

"Well, they do." I sell my lie well.

"But . . ."

"Be quiet. I've heard enough." I put my hand up again. She stops trying to talk. "Look at me. Listen carefully. You're going get yourself in trouble. You think you can use us to get back at him, but this isn't the first domestic dispute we've been to. We know when they are legitimate and when they are not."

She tries to speak, but I raise my hand again.

"Just listen for a moment. I've listened to your lies, now you listen to me. I'm going to give you good advice," I say. "You make up a charge on him tonight, he's going to make up a charge on you tomorrow. You're going to get a worse criminal record than you already have. You're young, you're pissed off, and you want to get back at him, but you're not going to use us to do it. Understand? Now show us a bit of respect and admit he didn't hit you."

"Well, he was going to and he has before," she says.

"Yeah, well, he didn't tonight and you just admitted it. There is nothing that even merits a case report. We both know that." I turn toward her baby's daddy. "Look at him. He's a goddamn idiot," I say. She looks over and smiles.

"You want to get back at him? Get your act together. Work. Get a decent apartment, a decent boyfriend. But don't play games with us. The law can go either way. If he alleges you hit him, I'll lock both of you up and let the judge sort it out. Remember, domestic charges mean you have to stay in jail overnight. You won't get out until late tomorrow morning," I say.

As I am speaking, Jan nods her head. The woman, still nervous from admitting she lied, listens.

"Here is what I'll do for you, even though you've shown no respect toward us. I'll tell him to get lost tonight and if he shows up again, I'll lock him up. I'll put the fear of God in him."

She waits.

"All right," she says.

He is still standing away from us next to the squad car, worried he is going to jail.

"I think that is the best thing to do. You just have to get this guy out of your life rather than fight him," I say, quite certain she never will.

"Yeah," she says.

"Thanks a lot, Officer. She was lying," her boyfriend says as we walk him away from the building a few moments later.

I turn and face him, violate his space. "Listen to me. If you come back here tonight, we're going to lock you up. No questions, nothing. Look at yourself: a grown man, borrowing money from the mother of your baby. It's totally pathetic. If you come back here tonight, you are going to jail. Understand?"

He pauses, considers a challenge, then nods. He turns, walks slowly down the sidewalk, bent forward into the wind, his hands back in his pockets, the hood of his sweatshirt covering his head. We walk back to the warmth of the squad car.

The car is filthy, the street dirty with melted snow. The drivers of illegally parked cars—waiting in bus stops or double-parked outside of small grocery stores—avoid eye contact when we pass. We are on Devon Avenue again. On this street I once arrested a working guy for possession of cocaine I found while frisking him, a small amount wrapped up in a dollar bill. It was left over from a Friday night and he had forgotten about it. He turned to me, looked me straight in the eye, and asked if I could let him go. And I would have, but a sergeant and that night's partner—not Jan, a younger partner who locked up everyone—had seen it. I took the guy in that evening, knowing he would spend the night there and take the bus in the morning to court with dozens of real offenders.

As we drive down Devon Avenue, I mark the side streets where I have picked up dead bodies, called ambulances, waited impatiently for the woman to stop sobbing so she can give me a description. I sense even now the quiet hatred people along this street feel for me, their contempt, their grudges against me. The law takes me into the filth and anger of the city, suffusing me in enmity.

I remember working alone one day driving down the north alley of this street, searching for cars driving slowly on their way to buy drugs from the dealers hiding on the porches. I watched a car cross several blocks down the narrow alley, behind the Indian and Pakistani restaurants. As I walked up the driver, a woman, leaned out of the car.

"What the fuck you pulling me over for? I didn't do nothing."

I had no intention of writing her tickets if I concluded she was not working for a gang. I could not finish a sentence.

"You stopped me 'cause I'm black. That's why. What the hell did I do driving that you stopped me? Bunch of fucking bullshit."

There was no way I could see the race or sex of the driver. I tried to respond, but each time she yelled over me. Fucking this, fucking that. I gave up.

I leaned closer to her, grabbed her license from her hand.

"You want to know why I pulled you over?"

"Hell yes, I do."

"I'll write it down for you," I said, and walked back to the car.

When I returned with two tickets, I pointed to the two charges on them. "Here. If you have any more questions about them, you can ask at your hearing, the date and location of which is here."

"Motherfucking police got nothing better to do than write bull-shit tickets for nothing," she screamed as I walked back to the car.

I pulled the squad car next to hers, rolled down the window. She was still cursing and screaming in the alley. I stared at her for a while, stone-faced while she continued her rant. Anyone could hear her.

"You kiss your baby with that mouth?" I asked her when she finally stopped to breathe, then pulled away, her rant resuming.

After this memory and so many like it, I question my affinity for this solitude, question the cost paid to get to the city in a manner where it opens up to me and I can think about it. There is no denying its force. I resign myself to the fact that it is something I inhabit without fully understanding. For better or worse, I cannot tell. In victims and offenders, witnesses, strange partners, my own lineage, I see the consequences of delusion, yet see also how false assumptions are almost unavoidable. I force myself into the daily facts of the city, measure and judge them, then reflect on them. This solitude, I wonder, is a way of staying coherently in the world—no small gift. I liken it to what professors once told me was the force in art called realism, an insistence on encountering the world as it is. I believe this solitude has this force, forces me to linger among facts and empiricism, delivers an authenticity that does not cringe or equivocate under point of view, consciousness, or self-pity. It is a foothold into the world, the world that can be pointed to and touched and, perhaps, described. The power of delusion is diminished, for such perspective places the city in context, providing a form and weight to all things.

Do I stay on this job in order to see without delusion? I make no efforts to leave it, though I often curse it, despise it. I do not take promotional exams. I often tell Jan I could not see myself working as a cop in any other city. Is that it, then? I am not so sure. Even after five years on the job, fifteen in the city, I cannot see where I am heading.

This solitude has been with me a long time, intensifying as I age. Standing on busy corners as a doorman fifteen years ago, I could sense it. I could claim it was only temporary; I was just making rent. But those short-lived jobs lingering on corners lasted years. Looking back now, it is as if those jobs were only hesitating steps toward a solitude I now inhabit almost constantly, with a greater intensity, and more darkness. As a doorman on the Near North Side, I could romanticize the city, pat the back of the tourist eager to drop his money here, show him the drunken city, the cultured city. Notes piled up even then. Already I was changing shapes, modifying speech. Soon I was writing grievances to the union for housekeepers, watching the Irish union bosses closely, standing outside employee entrances with pamphlets, newsletters, running and losing union elections, looking carefully before I ascended my back steps at night.

Now I remain completely within city limits, reflecting its bellicose sections, uncomfortable outside of it, unwilling to travel beyond.

I pull out from the curb. The street is full of pedestrians and traffic. Middle Eastern and Indian restaurants line the street. Cabdrivers are parked there, getting dinner. Up and down the street, no one is speaking English. Signs are in foreign letters. I am suddenly aware of my loneliness, aware that after all these years these notes never take form, never seem to become anything. The real city, I conclude, frustrates form. It is only kneading me into disjointed shapes, making infrastructural elements like my spinal disks and muscles weak and vulnerable. I have tried to make these fragments work, tried them as facts, as stories. Nothing. Once I resisted this solitude, scolded myself that it was a waste of time. Now I gear my life around remaining in it without knowing why, without any certainty, without, even, any form. It is perhaps the only thing I have truly cultivated. This loneliness turns to desolation. I have sacrificed, tossed away too easily, perhaps, so much for it.

A few minutes later, I catch Jan's eye in the car, both of us silent for a long time. "I'm just trying to get my life together." She smiles, thinking something along the same lines about her own life, her failed marriage, the lawyers, the custody battle, her son's father.

Jan recounts the details of her bitter divorce, and I shake my head at her husband's tactics. Then she moves on to her son, telling hilarious stories of his development, new words, concepts that have come to him. She bursts with a mother's love as she recounts them.

She tells of giving him time-outs, and after a pause I can't resist anymore. "You know what, Jan?"

"What?" she responds suspiciously.

"I think time-outs are a good idea. What we'll do is, I will give you a time-out after one of your outbursts. Lord knows that happens enough. You'll have to sit in the car while I count to thirty."

"You jackass."

"Uh-oh, disrespect of your partner. Time for a time-out already," I say, then begin counting slowly and loudly, putting up a finger and raising my eyebrows to let her know she cannot speak. "One . . . two . . . three . . . four . . ." She looks out the window shaking her head until I reach thirty.

"Okay. Finished. I'm excited about this. I think this is an effective BMS: Behavior Management Strategy. You feel better now?"

"Oh, you're gonna get it. That's it," she says, but she's laughing.

We drive for a while without speaking more than a word or two, through the Jewish area, the Latino, the Indian, and the black areas. Our district is the most mixed in the city, sometimes changing block by block. Jan has a sympathetic ear, listens when we go to calls, listens to me. On a few quiet nights over the winter, I've even told her a little about realism, told her this force—confronting the world as it is, finding out what it is—is what attracts me to American writers. I've told her many nights in the car how working the Civil War hospitals almost killed Whitman, but also formed him as a writer. I've explained that when Melville wanted to write an epic, he returned to the whaling industry, even though he already had mutinied from two whaling boats. I have told how these labors provided them with insight they could never ignore, their dark labor a means of seeing clearly. They were forced to acknowledge things as they were, even though such an insight posed all kinds of problems, especially with form.

"Yeah," Jan says, and I know she is listening.

I want to go so far as to tell her that this solitude I live in is a mark of finding that realism, a consequence of it, but I wouldn't know how. I barely know myself, though I want to, though I am working hard at it. I don't mention, either, what this solitude imparts, the strange insight into the city. I now marvel at the morning paper, infusing the obligatory stories with color and detail, much as I pick up submitted case reports in the bin and read the narratives, culling more authentic images than is stated in the established forms. Some of my best sentences on case reports arise in my mind.

"The following morning and throughout the next day, the victim observed several other peculiarities that, taken together, compelled her to consider that she had been the victim of date rape."

"Due to contradictory statements, admitted bias, absence of witnesses, unsupported claims, and utter unlikelihood of above events, Responding Officers remained intensely incredulous as to the veracity of the victim's statements, and therefore declined to make arrest."

My mind races to the addresses in the newspapers and case reports. I've worked there. I know that building. I imagine the sounds and smells. I can identify liars so easily now, admire the cops who can spot them even faster. I listen better than ever. I am more literate, more succinct; my thoughts are freer. I also want to tell Jan that the knowledge garnered in this solitude is my claim I am not static; my girth and weak back, my curses and obscene humor are not the result of indolence. They are signs of my becoming, my immersion in the city.

Yes, possibly, but becoming what? I compare then and now: myself now, moving steadily along the streets in a squad car, walking late at night into strange apartment buildings, with myself twenty years earlier, riding the trains and lingering along Lake Michigan. How deaf I was. What danger I was in. The sounds and images of the city shocked and baffled me. I tried to obfuscate them. I heard shouting one morning in the studio apartment I had lived in for almost a year. I thought it was a tortured cat or an old woman. I went from window to window and looked out my back porch at the streets and sidewalks below, but saw nothing. Following the sound to my bathroom, I pried open the window for the first time there and looked out. There was an old man on the top porch of the building next door, waving his hands and shouting. His clothes were filthy, his shirt open and his pants hanging down. I could see him between the leaves of a tree moving in the wind. Our eyes met and he tried to yell something to me. I could not make it out.

I went next door and saw for the first time the small sign in front stating this was a nursing home. I had never noticed it before. How many times had I walked in front of that building? I righteously demanded to speak to someone in charge, marched back home, and called the city Department on Aging. There are nursing homes like this one all over the North Side. They are as elemental to the neighborhood as its schools, police stations, nightclubs, and restaurants. Now I enter them every day to document the residents as dead, missing, or injured. I watch them sit in the cafeterias, illuminated by vending machines and fluorescent lights, the smell of urine everywhere. Often, while my partner fills out the paperwork, I walk down the halls and look into the rooms, two people in each one, the TVs loud. I read the names outside the room and perceive with one glance if family members visit, if grown children faced the anguish of placing their parents here, or if they were placed here by some action of the state deemed official and legal, much as many of my actions now are. I listen to the dialects of the workers—African, Filipino, Latino.

Lady in nursing home said she wants to leave but staff won't let her. Jan and I sigh after reading the narrative on the computer screen. It is some two hours into the tour, completely dark. I head north, taking a side street most of the way. Jan will let me speak at this one. When we arrive, there are nervous workers, guest workers they are often called now, Filipino, at the desk. I greet them politely and try to put them at ease. I look over at a large room with several TVs playing and a woman in a wheelchair is awkwardly making her way to us. I walk over to meet her in the large room.

"Hello. My name is Officer Preib. Did you call us, ma'am?"

"Yes, I did, Officer."

"What's wrong?"

"Well, they say I have to stay here," she says, pointing slightly to the nurses at the desk. "I do not want to be here. I have an apartment on Sheridan Avenue. I've lived there for twenty years. My husband died recently and I want to go home. They can't keep me here." Her voiced is filled with frustration, fear, and anger. It is a familiar. I remember my mother's slow demise.

Her arm is wrapped in a cast and she has bruises on her face. Likely she fell down in her apartment, I conclude. She has a hollow look about her eyes, the vacancy of a lifetime of alcohol. To relax her, I sit down at the table next to her and ask her questions about her apartment, how she came to be injured.

She worked in entertainment, doing voice-over commercials while her husband worked as an actor. They lived in a small, cheap apartment. After he died, she spent even more time alone there, probably drinking more, I surmise. I let her speak for a while and listen carefully, then tell her I am going to talk to some staff members about her situation. She looks at me so hopefully, so gratefully, thinking I may get her out of there that evening. Before I leave, she tells me she is supposed to have a meeting with the director of the facility in two days. My heart sinks, seeing her so hopeful. I doubt she will ever go home.

The Filipino nurse waits for me nervously, not knowing what trouble I will make for her.

"Did they determine she can't live alone anymore?" I ask quietly.

"Yes, they did. She has to stay here at least for a while," she says, admitting with the "at least" the strong probability she is no longer able to live alone. The nurse shows me her file, the short narrative of her fall, injuries, and the end of her freedom.

"There is a meeting in a few days, isn't there?" I ask.

"Yes, on Monday."

"The doctor will fill her in on her condition and when she can go home, right?"

"Yes, he will," she says, relaxing.

I am still reading the file, seeing a sentence at the end with the phrase "chronic alcohol abuser."

I sit down next to her again. I repeat the story of how she got there, recounting the facts. With each one she nods her head. *Yes, yes, exactly.*

"Well, Mrs. Phillips. You are pretty scared right now, aren't you?"

"Yes."

"You are going through a lot right now, and it's tough to lose your independence. But these doctors and these people don't think you should be home by yourself with your injuries, and, to be honest, I don't either."

She raises her head to interrupt, seeing she is losing.

"Hold on." I raise my hand gently. "But that doesn't mean you can't turn things around. Once your arm heals and you get back on your feet, you can go back to the apartment. You could use this place and how much you don't want to be here as motivation to get better. Mrs. Phillips, these people don't want to hurt you. They want to help. But right now you could be in danger. They have to evaluate you, and in this meeting with the doctor on Monday, you can ask all the questions you want. He's not going to lie to you. It would be against the law, and he could get in big trouble."

She is listening to me explain away her independence. Even in such a terrifying situation, she is calm and trusting of me. There is a good chance she won't ever get out of here. I am a used-car salesman. I feel so sorry for her. A drinker, yes, but so what? Kind and gentle in nature. Now all alone. Now in this state-run nursing home. No Broadway anymore, Mrs. Phillips. No watching movies at home with Mr. Phillips. It's fairly certain now, isn't it? There will be no big break, no leading roles, no penthouse apartments. No children, Mrs. Phillips, to gather your belongings from the apartment, talk to the landlord, come visit you, and say, "Remember the time . . ." You will be as forgotten as can be and you don't deserve it.

Even so, I have an idea.

"I'll tell you what, Mrs. Phillips. I work all this week, including Monday. You sit yourself down the next few days and you write down every question you want to ask the doctor. When Monday comes, you make him answer them. If you feel you are not getting the answers you want, or if they are treating you badly, you call me on my cell phone and I'll come over. I'll make sure no one violates your rights or treats you badly."

"Will you?" she says with such gratitude that I choke a little.

I don't care if it's getting busy in the district tonight, if there are calls waiting. I sit back in the chair, indicating I am willing to stay awhile.

"So, Mrs. Phillips, what kind of acting did you and your husband do?"

Jan sits down, too. We stay an hour, ignoring the calls on the radio until her memories relax her.

It takes a while for the sadness of the nursing home to ebb. The movement along Devon also pulls me out of my funk. Bringing up Whitman and Melville helped diminish my desolation as well. Another call right now wouldn't hurt. I would like to enter a building I've never been in before. I want to talk to Jan a little more about these writers, tell her that "realism" is an insufficient term. There is something else I am trying to get at in these writers. What calls me to them is their strong conviction, a faith in their writing, a religious sense. I tell Jan that Whitman often said he wanted his poems to be a kind of New Testament for the New World. It is the force in his poems that most pulls me, and his insistence on faithfully articulating the world as he saw it is part of it, the one connected to the other. I want to tell Jan I believe in this conviction, but I don't know how. I can't make it clear yet. My terms are useless: realism, religion, conviction. I pull the car to the side of

Devon, along a no-parking lane. I write the terms on yet another scrap of paper. "Do they go together? Can a sign of the right realism be that it leads to this religion?"

I reread it, place it in my pocket. Likely I will forget it. Likely it will not even make it to my drawer. It will be washed away at the cleaners or tossed with a candy bar wrapper at the end of my shift. But for now it seems accurate and not the first time I have drawn this conclusion on fragments: there is a kind of faith that lingers in realism, a belief that knowing the city will lead somewhere beyond the city.

Jan never questions these sudden stops and remains quiet while I write. I see her out of the corner of my eye, then look at her after I finish. I take out a new card and write quickly.

"Unbelievable," I say. "All this time it was right there before me. I got it. It's so simple, so clear. Just three words."

"Really?"

"Yeah."

"Can I see it?"

"Sure."

I hand it to her and start to laugh as I watch her make out the words: "Kill Partner Tonight."

"You probably wouldn't believe this, Jan, but I am in truth a religious person," I say to her after I stop laughing and she no longer harbors a grudge.

"You're right. I wouldn't believe that."

"Oh, so you think I'm a godless, amoral infidel doomed to eternal suffering?" I say. Jan is Catholic.

"Pretty much, yeah," she says, looking straight at me.

"Thanks for that input."

"No problem," she says.

Then I tell Jan there is a kind of promise in seeing the city as it is. I tell her how Whitman stayed with realism, insisted on describing New York, the battlefields, manual labor, sex as it actually was, sometimes just endless listing that somehow worked. I tell her how that insistence posed such problems with form, how much he wandered and failed until he discovered his open verse. He stuck with it, sensed it would come.

"There is a deep courage in his poems. He was a tough motherfucker," I tell her, listing all the problems that burdened him, that would have distracted many writers. I tell her how his greatest force as a writer arose from the lowest experiences, as a nurse in the war hospitals. As I say this, I realize how wrong I was earlier. Realism does not frustrate form; it creates it. You just have to be tough enough to ride it out. The soldiers opened up to Whitman. They gave him blow-by-blow descriptions of the battles. As I tell her this, I recall the immediacy of how I see the city, the privilege of it, the confessions and laments, the threats and the terror of a gunshot victim about to die. I am in their homes. I know how to get them to talk. Such intimacy in the world cannot help but lead to original writing. It must be. It must.

So much possibility lingers behind this tenuous conclusion, a euphoria all out of bounds. I suddenly love the elemental city, am far too ecstatic at my existence. While working, this euphoria is tempered by the obligations of my job, but when this conclusion arises on a day off, it is barely manageable. On summer nights off, I shave, wear a clean shirt. I gather some twenties from my dresser, ride my bike through the North Side, down the lakefront path with so many beautiful girls. I stop at bars along the way. I love the sound of wooden floors as I walk in. I smell the beer and whiskey rising up. I settle into the stools, ecstatic a playoff basketball game is on TV. I smile, disbelieving that such places exist on every corner. I am dizzy at the wonderful choices of beers. Germany, Belgium, Ireland. "Welcome, welcome all," I say, my arms outstretched.

I want to turn to the stranger next to me, stare at him, and say, "Can you fucking believe it?" and slap him on the back. The announcer on the TV is so insightful, so articulate. He comments that big men—that would be me—should stay in the paint and let the game come to them. "Brilliant," I whisper. That's where I belong and that's where I will stay. I'll never leave the paint again. Ever. When my selection arrives on the wooden bar, I am almost crying. The plump bartender knows to let some run down the side of the glass onto the bar. I've never loved anyone more. "Thank you," I tell her, fighting back the tears.

"You know, I am in my middle ages, but I believe my best years are ahead of me," I tell her after the first taste.

"Is that right?" she says.

"Sure it is," I say, sitting back in the chair, unashamedly patting my belly. "I'm certain of it."

"It's important to have a good attitude," she says.

"Attitude has nothing to do with it. Conviction is crucial, and so is endurance. But, and I can't stress this enough, you must let the game come to you. Stay in the paint, for Christ's sake. By the way, you are the loveliest bartender I have ever met."

"Okay," she says, then walks to the other end of the bar.

"I beg your pardon, but may I try the Belgian wheat?" I call out to her, but she ignores me. "Never mind, then," I say.

Most of Jan's money goes to her divorce lawyer. Unlike most cops budgeting for a family, I squander large sums on good meals. Jan budgets her money. I encourage extravagant meals. We lumber out of the car. All night long we have seen the promises of respite in neon signs. I insist we get an appetizer, that she take some food home for lunch tomorrow with her kid. I eat heartily, seduced by the grilled onions on Vienna beef, chicken breast sandwiches, spring rolls, sweet and sour pork. We loosen our vests, turn down the radios. We sit hunched over our table, letting everyone know by every gesture that we do not want to be interrupted. We do not wish to talk.

After we are done, we sit back. Jan reads the ads in the paper. I am watching TV. I look up at her.

"Jan?"

"What?"

"'There was never any more inception than there is now / Nor any more youth or age than there is now / And will never be any more perfection than there is now.' That's Whitman. That's where I want to get. That's where I think I can get to," I say, still thinking of where this conviction may lead.

She nods her head and we fall silent again. I let the words repeat in my mind, admiring them, wishing they were mine.

The radio has died down in our car. We are waiting to hear the cars from the next shift are on the street, an indication there are only a few hours left on our tour. It dawns on me that I have told Jan all these things about form and American writers before. I have been making this speech for many years. It was once exciting; now it haunts me. I feel as if I have been dishonest to Jan. I begin telling her about the many writers for whom the breakthrough never comes, thinking, she knows, of myself. I tell her I think the beatniks were an example—deluded, making up new forms because they couldn't master any, thinking they were at the center of things when they weren't. They got religion wrong, realism, drugs. I tell her I know this because I hitchhiked across the country in part because of their writing, and I found out it was all lies. I tell her how many kids my age were seduced by the Beats in college, still are, that I think they did far more harm than anything, all the kids taking drugs, trying religions like new clothes, how they spurned discipline for false inspiration. There is some anxiety in my voice, a guy who talks about doing something rather than actually doing it, which is all the difference in the world, Jan, all the fucking difference in the world. Look at me in this car, middle-aged. When will my form come? It already has, I tell myself, feeling my stomach push against my vest, and I fall as quickly as I rise.

"Anyway, it's complicated," I say to Jan, ending it. She doesn't press me.

I know when she can no longer discuss her divorce, no longer can think about the daily drop-off of her son to his father in the parking lot of a McDonald's, her child pleading to stay with her, the fucking lawyers, the crooked judge who got his job because of family connections, this fucking rotten, crooked, goddamn fucking city.

We drive and I continue to fall.

I've stayed with this solitude, this narrow, unreliable angle into the city, myself, art. And now panic sets in. I do not know if it is a gift or a curse. I do not know if it shapes life toward some good or pulls it away from what might have been. Am I shedding myself in preparation for something? It may be I covet the solitude because it is all that remains; I have simply shed everything else or squandered it. It may be that I have moved solely toward it. I don't know. Have I falsely gambled?

"You know, Jan, I sometimes can't help but think I've made a complete mess of my life. I don't know anything and never will." I know once again what a great partner she is when she doesn't respond.

Down and down throughout the night, the car growing cluttered, our jackets now wrinkled from sitting in the car, a few more domestics, several stops of gangbangers in alleys, some guy with a knife. I do not mind this descent into the city now. I move away from my panic; I refocus. It doesn't matter if we have to stay late. Nights like this one, nights when I have Jan as my partner and there is a steady flow and my back doesn't hurt so much, I find an unlawful joy moving from crisis to crisis, walking into apartments and taking long gazes amidst the shouting, listening to the victims, perceiving authenticity or lies. Jan writes the paper; I plot the courses and drive. We communicate with gestures and one-word statements.

"Kitchen" is all I say at the next domestic, letting her know someone else is in the apartment.

At home the following morning, I will sit in my boxers and extra-large white T-shirt, staring at the wall and tracing the origins of this solitude through these fragments. I will begin by opening the bottom drawer where I have kept notes that began when I was a doorman, my first job in the city. The memory of opening a door onto a busy street corner will return, along with autumn colors, taxis shooting past me, long conversations with workers in the neighborhood: salesmen, housekeepers, businessmen, cops. I'll ask myself again what point these fragments, what value? I will respond that they are an accurate account of a life in the service industry, an economy that transformed the city in my own formative years. For that alone, I think they hold value. But this conclusion, however accurate, will not satisfy. The fragments I crave, the ones I would string together, move from observations, the straightforward facts of Chicago, to insights more illuminating, revelatory even. The fragments I protect, though rooted in the city and accurate, go beyond the misery and mundane facts from which they arise by providing greater meaning, more possibilities, more complexity—a thrilling prospect. Their value? I will ask again. None, I must confess, unless the form comes.

We sit idling along Albion Avenue. Jan talks on the phone again. I am scribbling something that dissolves as I write, makes no sense. I sit back in the dark car, illuminated only by the computer screen, half listening to her conversation. I put my hand on the computer and begin to type a sentence on the computer screen, knowing she is watching.

"Ask him if he is well hung," I write. Jan steals an icy glance.

"What?" I whisper, holding my hands up. "You know how important that is to you."

I type over the last message: "Does he like sex in squad cars?"

Jan smiles, shakes her head, turns toward her own window, fed up with me.

I can no longer hide my origins, be ashamed of my girth: I take respite in the real city. I look around the dirty squad car: some bottled water, the wrapper of cheese popcorn I have sworn off many times, ticket books. I steer the car for a block with my stomach, searching for my cell phone.

I remain within city limits, suspicious of ideas, skeptical of categories—any abstractions that do not rise within its borders. I am committed to its laws, its manner of doing things. My liver is overworked, my stomach muscles weak. I will go to the YMCA to swim but only last five laps before I lean back in the Jacuzzi, my toes resting on the opposite ledge. I am tired of my guilt and regret, tired of considering my misery. In truth, I clutch my negative capability. I have let the city form me. There is a joy in it, a strange creative force, pulling me into its blood and guts, hinting at angels. I will go with it, push it further and further.

We are on Clark Street when we see the taxi pulled over, hazard lights flashing. We see the three yuppies on the sidewalk and the African driver. These yuppies are part of a gentrification of the neighborhood, turning vintage apartment buildings into condos. We arrive before the call comes over the radio, and we already know it is a cab dispute before the dispatcher announces it. Theft of services. As we pull around, another beat car pulls up.

I know Jan has no patience for yuppies. Her father abandoned her when she was little. Her mother raised them on the Northwest Side, poor working class.

The cabdriver stands uneasily next to his cab, leaning on his open door. Through the back window we can see the meter, frozen at $16.20. He is afraid of us. There is a lingering antipathy between police and cabdrivers, the cops angry at the aggressive driving of the cabs, their accidents, their licenses and insurance papers never correct. This driver fears we will side with his passengers simply because he is a cabdriver. The three yuppies, two females and a male, are dressed up for a night out and obviously drunk.

I walk toward the driver, ask him a few questions to confirm this is a fare dispute. He waits for my questions. He is reasonable. He answers in a thick African accent I must break down slowly to understand.

"Where did you pick them up?"

"From a bar on Lincoln in Lincoln Square."

The fare seems about right.

"Where do they want to go?"

"To Glenwood, around the corner."

"Why don't they want to pay you?"

"Because they said I went too far, but I came down this street because it was faster, only a block or two farther." Almost unintelligibly, he begins to describe why one route is better than another, pointing to the various directions he would go as he speaks, his hands waving, voice rising.

I interrupt. "So we're talking about seventy-five cents' difference in fare?"

"Yes."

I walk over to the yuppies. As I approach, one of the women walks toward me, drunkenly raising her arm to point at the cabdriver, and comes rudely close to my face.

"I want him arrested," she demands. "He took us out of our way and tried to increase the fare."

"You better put that hand down right now," Jan says decisively. I look at Jan and raise my eyebrows, reminding her with my glance that arresting them will make for a long night, with lots of paperwork. An officer from another car has procured IDs from everyone. I give them to Jan so she can run them. I calmly ask the drunken woman what happened, as if I am interested in her side, but my mind is already made up. She has to pay. I nod my head calmly as she rants, raising my eyes a few times and saying quietly, "Take it easy. I'm listening," hoping that she will run out of air, calm down. Instead she states over and over that she is a teacher and very educated. Her voice is loud, abrasive, condescending. The educated part is thrown at me as much as the cabdriver. It dawns on me that this cabdriver can probably speak at least two or three languages. I want to look at her and tell her that a monkey could pass education classes.

"Ma'am, honestly, your education has no bearing on this situation, and I'm tired of you shouting at me. The law is clear here. You have to pay the man for his services. It's theft. If you want, you can make a complaint against him with Consumer Services, but you have told me nothing at all here that would justify a complaint, in my mind. I don't think you would get anywhere with it."

As I speak, she sees we are not with her. Her ire grows. Her friend walks up to us as well. I put up my hand, tell her to stand back, but she approaches anyway.

"I'm not paying anything," the first woman says. "You don't know what the fuck you are talking about. This is bullshit. I've got more education in my finger than you'll ever have." As she says this, she puts her pinkie finger up in the air, and she shakes it inches from my face.

This is too much, even for yuppies. I stare straight into her eyes, take the moment to its crisis.

"Pay the man, or go to jail," I say.

She only rushes closer, along with her friend, waves the hand in my face again.

"Fuck you, you fat-ass pig," she says. "I got more education than you'll ever have. I teach inner-city kids on the South Side."

This statement draws furious chuckles from all of us standing there, it is so ridiculous. She sees us laugh, perceives our disgust at her foolishness, and her rage grows, the curses, the waving of her finger.

I look over at the officer next to me, an easygoing Irish guy with a family.

"Should I?" I ask him. He knows I am asking if I should I lean my head down to the microphone.

"Squad, can you send the wagon over here and another unit?"

He knows how I could calmly pull out a pile of complaints, walk over to the taxi driver as the three baffled yuppies watch me, and tell the driver to sign each one. I would hand them to Jan, walk back to the yuppies, pull out the handcuffs, and wheel them through each other, the clicking noise the first ominous sign that someone's life is about to change. I would guide the mouthiest of the yup-pies—the most educated one—against the car with my arm, force her arms around her back, and loop mine under hers, leaving her completely in my control. I would then taunt her with a few cold facts as her alarm rises.

"Education? Let me show you what I know."

Then the wagon would emerge stupidly from a side street, un-hurriedly lumbering toward our gathering, capturing the full atten-tion of our think tank. It would stop closely, the engine drowning out our radios, forcing us to turn them up. The wagon guys would come out, older, heavier than I, and perhaps even less educated.

They would look at the yuppies, then look at me, a little per-plexed.

"They gotta go. No choice," I would say, and they would nod. Okay. No problem.

The doors thick like a huge refrigerator would squeal as they open, the inside all metal and no windows to look out.

Likely the main offender would still be snarling as Jan searched her, outraged that she would undergo such humiliation, but the first glance inside the wagon would give her pause. When it does, I would lean close to her ear.

"You know, that's where we carry dead bodies to the morgue," I would say.

I would grab her and lead her in, force her to sit on the steel seats, then push the bar down, forcing her backward, her arms behind her back.

I know that by now she would begin crying and I would shut the door, taking my time with the case report and complaints, knowing the isolation would unnerve her even more. When I would open the door again, she would be begging. I know she would. They always do.

"Sir, I'm sorry. Can we forget about this?"

"Too late. The cabdriver signed complaints. I have to arrest you."

Then I would ask her if she was still on probation at her job. She looks and speaks as if she has not been teaching long.

"What?" she would say.

"Are you off probation on your job?"

"Not yet. Why?"

"I didn't think so. Well, I'm going to copy the case and arrest report and fax it to the superintendent of schools so he can see what kind of employee he has, drunk, stealing, and cursing out the police. Perhaps it may influence their decision on whether to keep you or let you go. I'm wondering if I should also charge you with assault for charging at me."

I would start to shut the wagon, and again she would beg.

"Sir, please, I just started. Can't you just let me go? I'll pay the driver."

"You're so much more educated than us cops and that poor cabdriver. You should figure a way out, right?"

I would hook her to the wall in the processing room after her humiliating walk into the station from the wagon, let her hear the prisoners coming and going, let her see the kinds of people living in the city. I could keep it up for hours, telling her it was a felony and she would be in county jail for seven days.

"Maybe you will run into some of your students there. You could play cards," I would joke.

But I don't.

"She fucking deserves it," the Irish cops says.

We divide the three. I pull the male to the side, ask him if he wants the other two to go to jail, and he starts to see the light. He walks over and insultingly shoves the money in the cabdriver's hand, all the while the two women continue to taunt us. *Pigs, fat ass, stupid.* The driver nods a thanks to us, gets in his car, and leaves.

I look up and down the street: at least ten Mexican restaurants, a few friendly to us, tire repair shops, a McDonald's, a few hookers enjoying the show, a few parked cars. Jan and I are still fuming as we get back into the car, second-guessing our mercy, the yuppies' claims of education ringing in our ears. I recall a night when, during a traffic stop, Jan suddenly broke into perfect Spanish.

"Where did you learn that?" I asked her afterward.

"I took it as an elective at the city college and just fell in love with it," she said. Now she is called to translate all over the district.

I confess to Jan I've been to five colleges. I describe the cycle of working menial jobs hoping to move up, prosperity, then, disgusted, returning to school to read literature. I tell her one of my happiest periods was giving up a decent job, going back to school, and studying classical Greek. The subject was so difficult, I couldn't work much. I lived in a basement apartment, got up every morning, and studied for three hours, then went to class, studied more afterward. Often I didn't even have money for coffee, but I was thrilled with the challenge of translating, blown away by the classical writers. Soon, though, the school required the declaration of a degree and demanded I take required classes.

There was the teacher who put a check mark next to my name

without looking up when I told him I hadn't read the assignment that week for the History of Christianity class I took in a large lecture hall. The doddering professor assigned his own textbook, and condescendingly interrupted his lectures and pointed to the class.

"Is there anyone who can tell me where Michelangelo's David statue now resides? Is there anyone who can restore a little faith in your generation?" he would say, his limp finger swaying in a large arc across the hall.

"Ah, there's hope," he said when a woman answered correctly from the back.

One day he was talking about some battle involving a French general. He paused, looked out across the hall.

"Is there anyone who knows what famous French dish arose from this battle?"

No one answered for a moment. I smiled. "French toast?" I said from the fifth row, then broke into uncontrollable laughter and walked out under his angry gaze. I got a C, enough to pass and get a degree.

Jan and I turn west on Devon Avenue. In the daytime, Muslims and Hindus line the street, many of the women covered head to foot. A little bit north are the Orthodox Jews who have lived in the neighborhood for decades. I've gone into their homes to complete reports and seen the foreign scripts on the bookshelves, the devout prayers I cannot understand. As we leave the homes of blacks, they often say, "God will provide," in response to the misfortune that brought us there. Latinos gather on Sundays in storefronts converted to Pentecostal churches. Toward the lake is the Jesuit university, where the yuppie teacher likely studied. No one is out now. No lights are on.

Amidst all these promises of revelation, a familiar loneliness creeps in. Even at my age, I cannot make out clearly the objects of my own veneration, nor their origins, a fact that fills me with anxiety. Even rejected things return, suddenly compelling, then suddenly dead again. My anger and disgust at the yuppie transform to pity, as I recall my own struggle to separate the real from the unreal, the sacred from the profane. Haven't I hurled drunken curses on the street? Haven't I prattled on about the unexamined life?

At the same time, I cannot deny my own conviction, the belief that these objects exist and wait for me. In this conviction I have confidence I will recognize them, handle them with requisite care; they will not be, as so many things were before, shallow and artificial, secondhand, like life through books. (I do not live by books now, am hardly informed by them anymore.) I sense these objects linger within city limits and that they are the real aim of my labor, for I observe that my immersion in the real city also brings me closer to them. Within city limits, I believe nothing, believe everything. I deny the disease of myself, instead let the city remake me, forgo the doomed journey for happiness, am content merely at the possibility these objects may exist.

After a short silence, Jan reads my mind. She suggests we get gas before we head in, ensuring no late calls that will force overtime, no flipped cars with drunk drivers, no shootings, no more sanctified yuppies. She has to pick up her kid early the next morning. I want to rise with my fragments. I turn the car off next to the city pumps. It is completely silent for a few minutes. Through the rearview mirror, I see the attendant walk toward us, hear him open the gas cap. The car shakes a little as he forces the nozzle into the tank. He seems to sense our mood. He only asks for the mileage and my work ID in one-word requests. I gather up the garbage in one pile, my notes in another. Jan gathers up the paperwork, and we head in.

ESSENTIAL SERVICES

Each of us enters the roll call room alone and sits silently and heavily in our seat. Some nod to each other, but most of us keep our heads down or stare at one of the announcements that have been hanging on the cinder-block walls for years, as if it might reveal something meaningful after all this time. We place our bags on the table in front of us or on the floor next to it. Many lean back in our chairs, arms folded into vest covers, two pens in our upper left pocket. Other vest pockets are stuffed with index cards in three different colors, cell phones, and gum. After ten minutes, the side door opens. The watch commander, preceded by a sergeant, who carries a small stack of documents, enters the room carrying a large book from which he reads various announcements from the podium. When he is finished, he looks down at the roll call sheets.

"Roman."

"Yes, sir."

"Shaughnessy."

"Sir."

"O'Neil."

"Sir."

"Wrigley."

"He's in court."

"Carter?"

"Sir?"

"You got court notification, felony, Twenty-Sixth and California?"

"Yes, sir."

"McCarthy."

"Yes, sir."

A new guy from the academy, my partner tonight. I steal a glance over at him. He catches it, nods. I nod back.

As the watch commander speaks, the sergeant walks back and forth among us, handing out returned reports, letters, awards, and, possibly, notification of a lawsuit. Officers only look up when he hands them something. When the watch commander walks out, everyone rises slowly and walks out of the room, carrying their gear. Only necessary speech, made in low whispers, ends the silence.

I walk over and introduce myself to my partner that night, Joe, only a few weeks out of the academy. He is tall and speaks as if he were raised in the city. He is also nervous, I can tell, but polite and friendly.

Other cops speak in quiet voices.

"I'll get the radios."

"Do you want to drive?"

"Do you have traffic crash reports?"

The absence of real conversation signifies a change within the room, the district, the department, the city, the government, and, consequently, the world. Many cops could remember a time when noise so filled roll call that the watch commander was forced to raise his arms and demand quiet several times above the din. Then, every announcement generated barbs from the peanut gallery, particularly if the narrative of an honorable mention were read aloud. Pity that officer who came forward to accept it. His wisdom, his honesty, his alleged sexual attraction to animals, the veracity of the award, his ethnicity, all became the fodder of their spontaneous outbursts, the watch commander often joining in. All the officer could do was wave and nod, red-faced, as he walked back to his seat with the award for saving a life, finding a gun, or capturing a fugitive.

We walk out to the parking lot, a blast of heat hitting us after leaving the air-conditioned station, and our silence continues. Above us, to the left as we come out, is a large antenna, installed some six months earlier and activated just a few days ago. It is the reason for our silence. We walk slumped underneath it, not looking up, eyeing the numbers on the side of the squad cars for the one that belongs to us, pretending we don't notice the antenna, as if nothing is wrong. Searching for our squad car, I see the two round objects on the roof of many cars that have already generated the name "rabbit ears." They are connected with thick wires to cameras that sit near the top of the windshield inside the squad car. Mine will be outfitted within a few weeks. Microphones on either end of the camera record everything said in the car. Cops, by new order, are also obligated to carry mobile microphones in an upper vest pocket, next to their cell phones and gum.

I turn back and confront the new antenna hanging from the old building, a strange, surreal contrast. Times are changing. The antenna will grab the data at the end of each night from the boxes in the squad cars, one car at a time, each lined up behind another, resentfully but obediently coming to a stop under it. Here the cars will wait while the antenna grabs the information without asking us anything about the images, without inquiring from us what they may mean.

One day the antenna just appeared, sticking out rudely from the side of the building. It was as if a new imagination had been imposed upon us and it was agreed this imagination considered itself superior to ours. Its function was to review us. An announcement came down the same week the cameras were made active that any infractions discovered by them would result in mandatory "retraining and education" classes. Whatever minds gathered together on the other end of the antenna obviously believed they could train us, could teach us, and their sudden arrival and total surveillance of our duties indicated they clearly did not approve of the quality of our work. We gathered underneath the antenna the day it arrived, stared up to it as if we wanted to ask it questions. *Where are you from? What is your worldview? What do you think of the police?* It remained silent and superior. Sensing its antipathy, we thought of ways to kill it, analyzing the wiring and cables that gave it life, but we feared that too would be recorded. We insulted it with crude jokes, trying to get a rise out of it, but it remained arrogantly unfazed. Eventually, we walked by it without any eye contact whatsoever, our heads down, knowing it had the ear of the superintendent, the mayor, the media, and community leaders in a way we never would.

I turn back to the squad cars, dozens of blue-and-white cars scattered across the parking lot, Joe following me. Squad cars were once a source of safety and respite. The backseat is an enclosed space. The offender inside cannot open it. The windows are sealed, a mini jail. Once someone is placed in there, we can relax, as long as he has been properly searched. Many times his agitation ebbs back there and he finally answers questions. The computer between my partner and me allows me to gather the essential facts. When the twenty-year-old offender in the back tells me he has only been arrested, like, a few times, I can see he has, in fact, been arrested thirty-five times.

The squad car is also where a cop and his partner spend most of their day talking at ease, in security and discretion. I've listened to partners confess the disappointments of their marriage, their estranged relationship with children, their rage against the department and the offenders on the street. I've listened to them say it in the crudest, most violent speech available, and I've responded in the same kind. It is an essential freedom of speech partners share after confronting the worst of what the city manufactures. Among good partners, among solid officers, it is assumed that what is said in a car stays in a car. In the parking lot, I see about half the cars now have the rabbit ears on, this freedom gone, the conversation within possibly picked up and evaluated by the hostile minds recording it.

But the loss of privacy is not what troubles us the most. I remember sitting in the mandatory training session where the cameras were introduced a few months earlier, much like the many orientations I sat through when starting a hotel job. As I listened to the lies posited as justification for the cameras, I concluded again that the city suffered, and had always suffered, a failure of imagination. This failure was rooted in the city's political institutions, wherein various factions, with deep roots, ceaselessly vied. They struggled not for a collective, measureable, and therefore describable vision of the city that would allow its institutions to work in concert, or even to agree on what the city was, but rather for absolute supremacy above all other factions, at all costs. Those which rose to the top, as a condition of their supremacy, enjoyed the right to impose their own sordid imagination upon the rest of the city, including ours, no matter how contradictory or how unreasonable. These worldviews were asserted without elegance, but instead with a powerful intimidation. Many people living under its tyranny did not truly believe this worldview in the slightest, knew they lived in an absurdity. Even the ones posing it rarely troubled themselves about its truthfulness. Everyone therefore settled for something they did not believe. This was the failure.

All the cops in the training room knew that much of what we encountered, and therefore what we did, could not be tolerated by the camera people and their faithful, not because what we did was wrong or unjust, but merely because their power could not admit our worldview. It took this failed, malevolent imagination to paint us into the corner we now found ourselves. We knew that the worst cops in the city, taken together in the worst of their crimes, would not in the slightest compare to the worst of what the city produced. Nearly half the city bordered on chaos. Nor would these camera people ever, in their power, admit the cruel, cowardly role they played in this chaos.

As a service worker, it was a common predicament to be re-trained and reeducated, a fancy term meaning one must agree with management. Yes, fine, sure, the customer is always right. But now, as a cop, it was a sticky, hopeless entanglement, absent of any trust. I felt as if my imagination were being outlawed, and looking around at the other cops in the training session, especially veter-ans, I could see I was not alone. The instructors prattled on about the cameras being an asset to our safety and an aid in our court testimony. To us, it signified a bold reconfiguration of power, one with no good outcomes, whereby the branch of the city, us, that tied at least one tenuous line from the city's daily facts and hap-penings to its institutions was now itself moved away from this es-sential service. We are the last line of realism in the imagined city. We're supposed to be the cameras, providing more than random, disconnected images captured for malevolent purposes. We pro-vide context and perspective to the images we observe, collected from long experience and practiced skill and at great threat to our own well-being.

Now the camera people peddled their worldview without con-straints or opposition, reminding us again of their power in the leering, condescending glare of the cameras positioned above our rearview mirrors. As powerfully as it invaded our space, the cam-era people left our union contract lingering on the fringe of the city's business, another sign of our diminished significance in the city's vying factions. The cameras arrived in the second year of no contract between the city and the union. The previous contract also lapsed for years before an arbitrator forced the city and the union into an agreement. Throughout the stalemated negotiations, the city steadily increased oversight of the police. The city introduced a disciplinary policy, now years old, allowing any person to level any accusation against a cop that was automatically investigated. Every gangbanger who got arrested or disliked a cop, even a gangbanger still in his twenties with fifty arrests on his record, could make any allegation he wanted, without any threat of prosecution for perjury or false reporting. Most gangbangers swore to make the allegation before they even made it to the station on an arrest, baiting the officers from the back of a squad car.

"You can't arrest me. Shit. Motherfuckers. I'm calling OPS, then I'm going to sue you motherfuckers," they would rant.

Careers were being ruined, good cops spending their time answering complaints from sociopaths. Isn't it supposed to be the other way around? These complaints were tallied on an officer's employment record. Now the city was fighting a move for these records to be used in lawsuits against the police, not simply the very rare ones deemed true, but merely the accusation, any accusation.

I remember the last official complaint against me, coming in the late winter, a warm night that hinted at the summer to come. I was scheduled to work with a recruit, still on her training cycles. We were sent to a domestic battery, the caller a woman, saying her husband was on scene and wasn't supposed to be there. The narrative sounded strange and I wondered out loud that it didn't sound right. On the way there, an update came over the radio saying someone had been stabbed. When we pulled up to the corner and got out of the squad car, the top window of a three-flat opened and a woman stuck her head out, saying her husband was in the building and shouldn't be there. She wanted him arrested. I leaned over to my partner and told her to keep an eye on the woman.

"I'll bet you she's our offender."

We walked up the stairs, hearing shouting from the top floor. As

I turned on the last landing, I saw a man wearing a doctor's garb holding his bleeding hand. He told us he was a dentist. Blood had soaked his clothes, ran along his arm, a trail of it going back into the apartment.

"Squad, can we get an ambulance over here? This is a bona fide stabbing," I said into the microphone.

The woman waited inside the apartment, shouting at me that she wanted her husband to go to jail because he came to their house and she had to defend herself. I didn't believe her. I told my partner to search her, ask her where the knife is. She wouldn't answer any questions. She handed me a mountain of papers, chronicling her doomed marriage, but no order of protection forbidding him from being there. Time and again I told her to be quiet, but she wouldn't listen. I knew she was trying to intimidate me from arresting her, but there was no choice. She stabbed the guy. I told her to turn around; I was going to put handcuffs on her. She refused. Would I have to use force against her? I leaned into the microphone.

"Squad, could we have another assist unit here?"

I got the cuffs on her, waited for another unit. When they arrived, I went back to the husband. He told me she waited outside a bedroom, then stabbed him. I approached her two children. The oldest one told me the same thing, that she stabbed him without reason and that the husband, the children's father, comes every weekend to the house. I also walked back to my partner, standing awkwardly at the kitchen table trying to fill out the case report. She had never been on a case like this before, but she was doing a good job, took directions well, was able to concentrate above all the shouting and chaos of paramedics, other cops, and family members.

I took the offender to the station. The entire time she was arguing we had no right to arrest her. I explained it to her a few times, tried to convince her it was in her interest to just ride it out. But she would have none of it. I looked at her through the rearview mirror.

"You ever been to the county jail?"

"No."

"Well, you just stabbed someone and your own son witnessed against you. That's a felony. It's up to the state's attorney whether they make this a felony or misdemeanor. That has a big influence on your future, so if I were you, I would calm down and become cooperative. You follow me?"

She started to see the point, finally shut up.

While we drove into the station, I heard my name called on the radio, answered up. It was a sergeant at the hospital, dealing with another stabbing that had occurred a few hours earlier on another beat. He asked me to come to the hospital and identify the victim. I had no idea what was going on, told him I would be there after I dropped off our stabbing offender.

"District is going nuts tonight," I told my partner, who nodded. I know she was stressed out. "Summer is going to be wild."

When I got to the station, I learned the guy I was supposed to identify is a known gangbanger. We had responded that night to a disturbance at a McDonald's where he and his cohorts had a fight with another gang. One of their members was stabbed in the back. Apparently, he had left his neighborhood and went onto their turf and been caught, stabbed repeatedly near a train stop. He died from the wounds. I heard this from other cops as we began processing our offender, who asked many questions about the fatal stabbing.

When I arrived at the hospital, I saw the victim on the gurney in the trauma room, his insides cut open and guts all over the room, blood even on the walls. The blood was bright red, almost luminescent, as if it still held some force of life in it that gave it such unreal intensity. I had never seen a trauma room so violent. I looked at his face, recalled his cockiness at the stabbing earlier in the day, when he refused to answer our questions. I identified him, then headed back to the station to our current stabbing.

This is what goes on in the city every day. This is the way it is. When the weather gets warm, there will be many days like this.

Three months later I get a notice of a complaint from our offender, claiming I had no right to arrest her, that I repeatedly mentioned a murder in the district that night as a means of intimidating her, and that I had threatened to charge her with a felony to intimidate her as well. I read through the complaint several times, count the months since the last time I received one, knowing that too many within a certain time period will result in mandatory training classes from some faction of the camera people. I sit in front of the computer screen to type out my response.

"What the fuck?" I write. "She stabbed her husband. Her own child witnessed against her. I locked her up. Now what is the fucking problem?" I reread it, erase it, a line from *King Lear* rising up in my mind.

"'Is it not as this mouth should tear this hand for lifting food to it?'" I write again, smiling.

I erase it. Begin again.

"I am submitting this report in response to the above complaint . . . ," I write, seething again. I cannot imagine how this complaint can exist, how it can be processed. I did what? Arrested her? She stabbed her husband. No one argues that. I intimidated her? That's my fucking job. I'm a cop, for Christ's sake. I shake it off. I need the job. I write my concluding statement.

"I am proud of my conduct and that of my partner on this evening," then submit it.

At first, the department refused a court order to release complaints against officers to the courts, but they eventually submitted. Lawyers, we knew, would fish through them, looking for any inconsistency, any detail they could use to build a case and generate a settlement. Offenders became more aggressive, more combative with the advent of the new policies. What was there to lose? In response, more and more cops were less willing to enter the worst circumstances of the city; that is, less willing to be the police. And who, the cops often grumbled in their bitterness, would enter it then?

Yeah, who?

Here in this wasteland, we remained, open to all kinds of malevolent and fraudulent accusations. The city barely even believed it had to sit down and hammer out a contract with us, even after our broken bones, fused spines, blown-out knees, compressed neck vertebrae, shattered hips, and a few of us dead.

The cameras would, inevitably, capture some malfeasance from a dumb-ass cop, stupid enough to commit his acts on a recording he already knows is there. But for the most part, cops are already conditioned to dozens of people turning their cell phones on them at a melee or when they use force to subdue an offender. Cameras from banks and stores capture many images. That's not enough, now. The camera people dig deeper. I have surreal images of brain implants becoming a condition of employment, so that they could review my thought processes in the course of my job. That would surely be the end of me.

In the training session, the instructors played two videos of the same incident from different vantage points, where police are chasing down an offender who refuses to obey them. In the first video, the officer suddenly raises her weapon and repeatedly fires at the offender, who falls and dies a few moments later. It looks like a willful execution. The second video clearly shows the offender raising his arm and firing a handgun, invisible in the first video, at the female officer's partner. She raises hers and fires back.

The cops realize from watching these tapes that no action or statement on record can admit of any ambiguity, yet ambiguity is a cop's condition, one it takes years to learn how to navigate. These ambiguities are seized by offenders and their lawyers to construct their own fiction, a fiction they often find quite lucrative. Even events of no ambiguity at all can find wild interpretation at crime scenes. At any police shooting in some neighborhoods, even when the offender is found with a gun that has been fired, when tests reveal powder burns on his hands, and when bullets are recovered matching his gun, residents come forward and swear, under oath, the police executed him with no basis whatsoever. Sometimes they claim the police handcuffed him first, then shot him in the middle of the street. Such claims are often repeated in the papers. No. The only reasonable response, the only safe one for cops in such a non-reality, is to fade back from such ambiguities, and many cops foresaw a career of writing parking tickets and moving violations right there in that training session, as well as seeing the city moving one degree closer to a violent absurdity.

The length of time the recordings remained at the computer center was a hot topic among the officers. This was the question that lingered throughout the first day of mandatory training. The instructors avoided it for a few hours, before someone finally raised their hand and asked point-blank. The instructors squinted when they said "forever," knowing the officers would erupt from their silence with a loud wave of protest and curses.

Get the fuck out of here.

What kind of bullshit is this?

The images lasted longer than the sentences of even the worst offenders. This imagination had perfect memory, preserving images that could be used by any realigned faction running the city in coming decades. As we were told this, each cop came to the same unspoken question in the same moment: *What about my pension? Will it ever be safe? Will I be called in Florida about an arrest twenty*

years earlier I don't even remember to be informed I have been indicted for
something that was commonplace during my career?

Most of us familiar with the workings of the city believed the real purpose of the cameras was to gather images against us; that the cameras were in fact another sign of a growing antagonism to our worldview. There were justifications for them. Several officers on an elite team were indicted for kidnapping drug dealers or breaking into their houses and stealing their money. Another cop was videotaped at a bar ruthlessly beating a female bartender because she wouldn't give him another drink. Another retired police commander faced ongoing accusations of torture against murder suspects some thirty years earlier. The camera people paraded these events into the media with an almost salacious frenzy. *See? See? See what they're really like?* Now the people on the other side of the antennas waited for more images, certain they were only the tip of the iceberg.

I follow the lines of my own imagination, weigh it against the ones now scrutinizing me. What I have become in the city is the product not only of seven years on patrol, but twenty years in Chicago. Further than that, really: my parents grew up in Rogers Park. My mother, upper middle class, loved the city for the opera, shopping, nightlife. She never wanted to leave, and after she did, she was never able to recover the city she lost. My father, more working class, fled the city because it always meant work. He grew up in an apartment, left, and returned only for a few months to the suburbs near the end of his life. My siblings never returned. They went west. Only I came back, and I am not sure why. I believe sometimes it was a terrible mistake, an overly retrospective force in my personality, tied to my father's constant disappointment in me. Or perhaps I shared my mother's sense that something was lost when I moved from Chicago.

Near the end of her life, I finally moved my mother back for a few months to the north suburbs, but it was too late. She was in terrible health and all her friends had died or were close to death. I remember her sitting in the lobby of her retirement apartment building on the North Shore, greeting people as they came and went, watching them, as if the old city she once loved would come along any minute. Then it dawned on me: I worked in hotels for many years as a doorman. Was I waiting for the same city?

I don't know. I only know the city held a mystery I could not name, but eventually allowed myself to be in. I let it shape my imagination. I don't apologize. When I returned here two decades ago, I fell immediately into the city's service industry and never came out. Whatever lessons I brought to the city quickly proved useless, and I had to begin largely from scratch, searching for my own way to compose whatever I found illuminating. Much of that composition will be passed along to Joe in the next few weeks in the strategies I impart to him, if things work out between us.

I look over at Joe as we load the trunk with the myriad reports and complaints. I've been training recruits for three years, on and off. I pause, remembering the cameras and the antenna staring rudely at me from the building. I sense that whatever I am, whatever I have become, seems repugnant to the imaginations behind these cameras, else why would they be here? They seem ambitious to re-create the city, and they sense our incredulous disapproval of their plans. Since becoming a doorman so many years ago and now as a cop, I am met with a hostility at dinner parties and barbecues with friends allying themselves with the camera people, and I often make excuses to leave early, sensing my increasing desire to recede from the gatherings of my professional friends. I shut the trunk, open the backseat to see if anyone left a gun or drugs there. I'm not sure if there is any point in tutoring recruits like Joe anymore, but I will, out of a sense of duty and deep feeling that these lessons are valuable, useful, and accurate—more valuable, and truer, than the motives and planned re-creations of the city by the camera people.

I imagine the camera minds reviewing tapes of my lessons, playing them two or three times before me in an interview room.

They pause the tape of me talking to a partner in the squad car.

"Do you always refer to members of your community as shit-heads?"

"Not all of them, but those guys I do."

"Don't you think that is prejudging them? We're going to advocate some retraining exercises on community interactions . . ."

The first few interactions with Joe tell a lot. He politely introduces himself to the other officers outside the radio room. He brings me a radio and hands me the keys to the car. He is tall and strong. By his bearing and his speech, I suspect he was raised in the city, perhaps street-smart, from a union family. But he also looks nervous, tries to anticipate what I am doing. When I look into the backseat, he opens the rear door on his side, as if to tell me he didn't forget to check it. Because he is nervous, I forgo my favorite joke of putting fake dog crap in the backseat when my trainee isn't looking. Then I would wait for him to open the door and point it out to me.

"Oh goddamnit," I would shout. "Now we got to fucking call Hazmat. Motherfucker." Then I would tell him we have to flip a coin to see who wipes it up.

But I'm in no joking mood. My mind can't leave the cameras.

"'What are the roots that clutch?'" I say as we pull out of the parking lot. I often quote favorite lines of literature and movies in the car.

"What's that?"

"Nothing. Just thinking out loud. You want to get some coffee?"

"Yeah, if you don't mind."

"Course not," I say, reassured by the kid's politeness, turning south on Damen Avenue to the Dunkin' Donuts on Peterson.

One thing I have learned during three years of training recruits is that it is better to show them the city than to tell them about it. We design our days accordingly, starting with elementary skills like the geography of the district, how to write tickets, and move into report writing, then to traffic stops, reading the information that pours out of the computer, and, finally, arrests. When not figuring out our own calls, I assist on others, so that Joe can see how other cops handle things without being distracted by processing it. After these calls, I will review them with Joe, asking what he thought was good and bad. This lesson of showing and not telling is a crucial one in a cop's life, for with his family (if they are not on the department) and friends, stories of city life are met with an incredulous stare, perhaps a polite nod of the head. Behind it the uninitiated listen with a skeptical voice, wondering that the storyteller must be somewhat jaded to concoct such tales, certainly to find such humor and pathos in such misery, cruelty, and absurdity. This sentiment plays a powerful role in the arrival of the cameras. They too find our reports and testimony fantastical, fraudulent. The first few years a cop spends trying to convince friends and other bar patrons that he is not exaggerating, but then he gives up. The distance between seeing the city in the real, as the cop does, and reading or talking about, the way others do, becomes unbridgeable. The point is that people call us, an inarguable sign that we are not making this shit up.

After coffee, there is an assignment of domestic battery, probably the most common call and always dangerous. We park behind the primary car, open the gate in front, and search out the address. There is the door, blocked open by the responding officers. We walk up the wooden stairs, hearing the shouting voices above. I step faster, take two steps at a time, so does Joe. I can sense Joe's nervousness as we approach. He is not sure of what to say or do. I remember the feeling on my first domestic batteries.

The narrative on the call stated a man returned from a fight with his girlfriend earlier that day and punched her twice in the face. As we arrive on the top landing, the responding officers already have the boyfriend, a white male, about twenty-five (too skinny, sunken eyes, drinker), handcuffed there, one officer standing next to him. The girlfriend, about the same age as the offender, with a wispy voice and sunken skin (another drinker: the bonds that unite), is standing just inside the open apartment door, answering questions from the other cop, who is hurriedly trying to write the case report. Her eye is already dark and swollen. He may have broken her eye socket, and she says there is a large blind spot on her peripheral vision. She may need plastic surgery. I can tell she has no medical insurance. A dog is barking somewhere in the building. I step up to the same level as the offender, from a lower step, stand next to him. He is still cursing out the girlfriend, calling her names, unacceptable in my mind, but it is not my call.

"You fucking bitch. I told you not to see him. This is my apartment, too. Fuck you, you fucking cunt. While I'm fucking away at work, you're just fucking around."

I take note of the fact that he has a job.

People open their doors to look out. The other officers ask us to transport him in to the station. They want to get him out so they can finish their report in peace. The offender looks at me as I approach him, unleashes his tirade against my partner and me, motherfuckers, pussies, the usual stuff. Joe, without prompting, stands next to him and places his hand under the offender's arm to control him. I like this kid. We start to walk him down the stairs and to the car, but he is squirming away from us as he yells at us.

"For a guy going to county jail, you sure got a big mouth," I say indifferently, bending his wrist until he complies.

"Fuck you, I ain't going to county."

"Fuck me? No, no, no. Fuck you," I say, putting my face close to his. "That's felony battery, you son of a bitch, and the way we're going to write it, you're going to county, so fuck you, you woman-beating piece of shit. I'll bet you five hundred bucks you've been arrested for domestic battery before. That's felony, too, so you're going to fucking county."

I realize right there if the cameras recorded me saying this, I would be reprimanded. We walk him down to the courtyard, then slowly to the car, eyes from the street watching us carefully. I open the back door of the squad car and nod for him to get in, but as I feared, he refuses, continuing to curse us out. I nod for Joe to watch him, and I walk to the other side of the squad car, this perhaps the oldest police move there is. Joe may as well learn it now. I climb through the backseat and reach out to his handcuffs, grab them, and yank. With his hands behind his back, he is powerless to resist and he falls into the seat sideways. Joe shuts the door and he is secure. We laugh a little. We get in and drive, the offender's tirade undiminished. My partner sits and listens, makes no comments. The offender leans back in his handcuffs, lifts his legs, kicks at the door and a window a few times. A broken window will be a mountain of paperwork. Then we will probably have to wrestle him down—more paperwork—and he may cut himself in the process, not to mention us—even more paperwork.

"Why are you beating up on that door?" I ask. "It's not a woman half your size."

Joe likes this line and we laugh. Our laughter infuriates him, and he begins cursing again, then kicks harder. I pull over, get out of the car, and open his door.

He looks up at me.

"I can send you to the county for the domestic," I say. "If you kick out these windows, I'll spray you with this fucking mace, then I'll double the felony charges so that you do double the time there." As I say this, I point to the canister on my belt. "You beat that woman up, not us. You, not us."

As I say this, I reach down to his collar and pull him close to me. He sits and stews. I let him sit there for a moment, and I stand next to him, his door open. Then, when he doesn't respond, I get back into my seat, close the door, and start driving, but not to the station. I go around the block, kill some time, because I know he is now thinking about losing his job by being at the county jail. I know the image of the county jail is rising in his mind.

"Officer, I'm sorry. I shouldn't have said what I said. I have to work tomorrow and she's driving me crazy. I just want to get out tonight," he says after a pause.

"Think about how you just acted toward us. Why the hell should I do anything for you? I want to put you in the county because that's where you belong for beating her that badly."

"I know, Officer. I know. I didn't mean it. Give me a break."

I know I've got him now. Much of what I've said is a lie.

"If you keep quiet, let the cops do the paperwork, and act like a gentleman, I'll see what I can do," I say.

By the time we get to the district, he is quiet, calling us "sir." He asks every few minutes if he is going to the county, and I keep repeating, "I don't know yet. We'll see," hanging it over his head. He doesn't know that in Cook County she would have to be nearly dead for him to be charged with a felony. We casually converse with him while starting the paperwork for the other officers, advising him to end the relationship.

"You're right," he says.

They charge him with misdemeanor domestic battery. We walk down the hallway, back to the squad car. I know Joe wants to talk about the call. I tell him I went right to the county jail threat because he mentioned a job in his tirade against the girlfriend. If he has a job, he has something to lose, so I held it over his head. Also, the fact that he works means he is not a total mope and is probably not familiar with how someone ends up in county, so I bluffed. I knew he dreaded going there. The mopes know it is a miserable place and that they will be there possibly seven days. Most guys expect to be released the same night on a misdemeanor I-bond. He knew the girlfriend wouldn't pursue a case against him, probably wouldn't even show up for court, so he thought he was home free. I had to dispel him of that notion and say it in way he found convincing.

Joe nods.

I tell Joe the most important thing is that you can't let guys walk all over you the way the previous offender did at first. You just can't. "What if we brought him to the station all worked up and let it get worse? He would start flailing in his handcuffs, probably cut himself, then he would need to go to the hospital. He might tell the doctor we tortured him and file a complaint. They do this shit all the time, Joe. We'd be here until four in the morning. We'd have to do a ton of paperwork. Even if he didn't cut himself, you never want to pass a prisoner to the lockup guys in a highly agitated state. Sometimes it can't be helped, but for the most part, you have to avoid it. It's professional courtesy. In any case, the police must maintain control. When you lose control, you are in all kinds of danger and you must find a way to get it back."

Now is as good a time as any to introduce the one thing I must teach new cops.

"The point is this, Joe: Always play your leverage on this job. Always."

I will repeat this imperative each day we work together and review stops and calls based upon it. Each move we make, I turn to Joe and ask him what his leverage is and how he will play it. Before we stop the car, I ask him why we are stopping it. By the third week, the end of his training cycle, I will remain silent on all calls, letting him handle them until he buries himself and then I try to help him out. He will carefully walk up to the gangbangers in their car and ask for a license. When the driver says he doesn't have one, Joe will pause, not sure what to say, then look at me for help.

"You don't have one on you, or you don't have one in general?"
I will take over from the passenger side.

"I don't have one at all."

"All right, I appreciate your honesty."

Now I play the leverage.

"You don't have insurance either, do you?"

"No, sir."

"You know I can take your car when you have no license and insurance. You got two hundred cash, because that's how much it will cost to get it from the pound."

"Please, sir. We're just going to a friend's house."

"Listen, I want you to step out of the car, but while you do, I want everyone else to keep their hands on the seat or dashboard in front of me. Don't fuck with me, gentlemen. I know who you guys are. I'll take the car and lock everyone of you up . . ."

And after I instill the notion of leverage, I begin telling Joe how to argue it, how to let it frame his speech. I tell Joe that maintaining control of one's speech is as crucial as anything. Losing it is often a prelude to larger, more physical dangers. It is not what people say; it is what they want from what they say. That's what you have to pay attention to, and each group within the district utilizes different tactics. Pointless to lecture further. Better to show. Joe and I start several days of traffic stops. We smell weed in one car. We take out three gangbangers, their eyes bloodshot.

"You guys smoking weed?" I ask.

"Why would I be smoking weed, Officer?"

There it is.

"Why are you asking me rhetorical questions?" I shoot back. "What the hell do I care why you are smoking it? I'm gonna ask you again, before I take your car from you. Have you been smoking weed?"

They pause.

"Yeah."

"Was that so hard? You got insurance on this car?"

The passenger chimes in. "Officer, we were just going to a girl's house. He doesn't know."

"Whoa, whoa," I say, putting up my hand, and look at the passenger.

"Are you his lawyer?"

"No."

"Then why are you interrupting me? I'm talking to this guy."

He puts his head down. I return to the driver.

The whole time, Joe looks at us blankly, not sure what is going on. I approach Joe. We debate taking him in. Having no ID, we will likely have to process him, fill out the many computer screens of information, then wait for approval from the desk sergeant, then the watch commander. He is also wearing a boatload of jewelry, which, under new order, must be inventoried separately from other possessions. Two hours? Three? Is the lockup busy and backed up? Besides, they cooperated. No, we'll cut him, the decision I make more and more these days.

Afterward, I review the conversation. I point out that the most common rhetorical trick among black gangbangers is to seize the conversation by aggressively asking rhetorical questions. That way, they have you answering to them and they steer the conversation away from what they are trying to hide. They hope to fluster you so much that you give up and cut them lose. *Why would I be smoking weed, Officer?* Almost any response that is not a question would put you on the defensive, leave him in control. I got the conversation back by asking him the same kind of question. Another tactic is for a member of their group to chime in and distract you, which, if it works, they will all start doing. You will lose your patience and they will have you on the run, a most dangerous position. You have to remember that you will be stopping some people over and over, like the gangbangers. They talk to each other about the cops in the district. When they get away with it once, they'll do it every time you stop them and word will spread. Soon they won't listen to anything you say.

Then I tell Joe how difficult large gatherings are with gang-bangers, how when you detain one guy and put the cuffs on, they will circle and start taunting you, claiming you have no right, screaming as if they are in shock at your actions. Their mothers will come running out, not to chide their kid for his behavior, but to violate your space. They will come too close to you, demanding to know why you have detained Sonny, even though Sonny is an adult and you legally owe Momma no explanation. Once she or the group gets you under their control and you start responding to them, being distracted by them, they will circle like wolves, hoping you will lose your focus. They will be ready with cameras on their cell phones photographing you. It will be used as the basis of a complaint and lawsuit if you say or do the wrong thing.

"You know how you maintain control?"

Joe looks at me, puzzled.

"You do to them what they are doing to you, and you always, always"—and I pause waiting for him—"play your leverage," he finishes the sentence.

"If they take control of the conversation with rhetorical questions, you take it back with rhetorical questions. That's why I asked him why he was asking me rhetorical questions. He had no answer, and the pause brought the power back to me. You should always be asking questions, not answering them. Then his friend piped in to distract me, so I cut him right off by asking him if he was his friend's lawyer, and went back to the driver, because that's where my leverage was."

Joe nods his head.

We stop a Latino driver in an old pickup truck a while later. The driver stares blankly while Joe asks for his license. The man mumbles no a few times so Joe tells him to step out of the car. Joe tries to ask more questions, but he continues to stare.

"Should I ask for a translator?" he asks me.

"Hold on."

I walk over to Joe. I stare into the car.

"Well, he has no insurance and no license, so we will have to impound the car." Then I look over at the man.

"You don't want us to impound the car, do you?"

"No," he says.

"But you don't have the necessary paperwork to be driving, do you?"

"No."

I look at Joe. "His English is getting better all the time," and again we cut him loose because he has a job and seems okay.

It is easy to work with Joe. He asks astute questions, so I decide to work a little harder with him. I head over to the gangbangers on Pratt and Bosworth, one building undermining the whole neighborhood. Street stops are now the most dangerous. The notion of probable cause in stopping gangbangers on the street is twisted in the courts, often times getting rejected. If the judge rules there was no probable cause, cops are left vulnerable to lawsuits for civil rights violations. Gangbangers know this; they refuse to obey orders from officers during street stops. They get out of hand fast, having little to lose. Five of them are now standing on the corner, no doubt working. I speed up to them, cold, with nothing. As I get out of the car, I see one approach, riding his bike on the sidewalk: my leverage.

"Come over here," I say.

"We ain't doing nothing."

"Come over here," I say.

They come over slowly, considering a refusal, always a tense moment. I watch their hands, their waistbands, recalling how a coworker once walked up on a guy pissing in an alley. The guy reached into his waist, pulled out a gun, and pulled the trigger ten feet way, but it only clicked, misfired. My colleague fell to the ground as he pulled his gun and began firing, but missed. The offender, who had just beaten a murder charge in court, ran down the alley. His partner jumped into the squad car and gave chase, shouting, "Emergency, shots fired," into the microphone. As the cop in the squad car emerged out of the alley, the offender jumped out from some trees, surprised him. The offender raised his gun and pointed it at the officer, who slammed on his brakes and jumped out of the car, ran to the other side for cover while the car rolled forward. He too heard the click of the gun as he ran, but it misfired again. The cop drew, pointed his gun, fired three times, missed, took better aim, fired twice, and hit the offender in the shoulder and arm. The offender then ran into an alley as my partner and I pulled up. The cop who had just shot the offender was so keyed up he could barely speak, pointing into the alley. We thought his partner was in there, so I drove slowly into it. We got out of the car, and I told my partner, two weeks out of the academy, to watch his line of fire, then we walked along a brick wall into the alley, me dreading coming around it into the line of the offender's fire. As I came around, I saw him bleeding on the ground, the gun next to him.

So now I scan them steadily, back and forth from their hands and waists, wondering if they will obey me. There are five gangbangers in this group, all familiar. We are outnumbered. I call the stop calmly into the radio.

"Twenty-four fifty-five.

"Twenty-four fifty-five.

"Street stop, Pratt and Bosworth. We're fine."

Joe takes one side of them on the car. Good. In addition to handling the stop, I have to monitor his reactions. Some young guys just stand there, frozen. I nod at Joe as I approach the first one and start talking to him. Joe understands, maintains a good position to guard. They start mouthing off, testing our reaction. They look at each other, start their own conversation.

"Police ain't shit."

"They got nothing better to do."

"They're all corrupt."

What creativity these guys will employ with the cameras soon coming their way.

They start laughing after each statement, then they refuse to answer questions. I know they want nothing more than for us to lose our tempers. I look at each one carefully. One of the gangbangers stirs my memory. He and three cohorts pushed over a middle-aged man who was riding a bike, laughed while they beat him, then took his bike. They could have just stolen the bike. The man, who needed stitches, had just bought a condo in the neighborhood. He sat in the station for two hours, the stitches on his forehead, his legs scraped and bloody from the fall, his bike clothes torn and ruined. He could not definitely recognize the offender, so the kid was let go, smiling, talking shit as he walked out of the front door of the district with his mother, who vowed a complaint for police misconduct. "What the hell for?" I couldn't help asking her as she walked by me. "Doing our jobs? Good luck with that."

I make an ironic laugh as these guys continue slamming the police, shake my head. I walk over to the guy standing next to his bike, grab it, and walk it to the car.

"You know that guy?" I ask the mouthiest of them, one who just claimed the police regularly steal from people, pointing to the one I just took the bike from.

"Yeah, he my cousin."

I look at the kid who was riding the bike.

"This your bike?"

"Yeah," he says.

"Mine now," I say.

"Ah, hell no. You can't take my bike."

"Wait, what?" I ask him. "I can't do what? You've got to be kidding me, telling me what I can and can't do. Are you testing me?"

"No, I ain't testing you. I just want my bike."

"You want your bike?" I repeat. I turn and look at the rest of them. "Now who has ID?" I say.

They stumble and mumble. I nod to Joe to collect their IDs. Two of the IDs are from the county jail. They just got out. After Joe collects the IDs, I move them away from the back of the car, reach into the driver's door, and pop the trunk. I walk over, pick up the bike, and place it in there.

"Officer, what you doing?" the guy with the bike says.

"I'm taking your bike."

"What for?"

"For many reasons. You're riding on the sidewalk, for one. This bike is also too small for you. Let me ask you a question. Without looking at it, can you tell me what kind of bike it is? The make and model?"

He pauses. I'm certain the bike is stolen.

"I didn't think so. Can you tell me where you bought and how much it cost?"

Silence again.

"I got it from my cousin," he says.

"I thought you said it was yours."

"Well, I meant . . ."

"Where is your cousin now?"

"I don't know."

"I don't believe you. Can you call him over here?"

Silence.

"That's what I figured. You're lying. So now, in addition to riding on the sidewalk, I think I am going to charge you with theft. In any case, we inventory the bike until you can prove it is yours."

I walk over to him, pull out the handcuffs, put them on, search him slowly and methodically, then lead him to the back of the squad car and into the seat. I shut the door, finished with him for now. I make sure to lock the doors, so if something goes off on the stop, his friends don't release him.

I take the names of all the rest of them, fill out the required cards whenever we stop someone. Then I pause, walk back to the mouthiest, lean close to him.

"How'm I doing? Am I passing your test?"

He is silent.

"What's the matter, nothing to say now? No wisecracks, no slam on how crooked the police are? We all know what you do out here. You must've been locked up twenty times by now and you're not even twenty-five yet. And you're telling me I'm crooked? I'm a thief? Where the fuck you get off talking to me like that? Who the fuck you think you're talking to?"

"You right, Officer. I'm sorry. You don't have to take my cousin."

"You don't need to tell me what I can and can't do," I say, control back to me.

I return to the index cards, intentionally taking my time filling them out.

"I'll tell you what. I'll let him go with a warning this time for riding on the sidewalk. But you owe me for it. One smart-ass response from you, any of you, when you walk away, and he's going."

"We won't, Officer. I promise."

We uncuff each one, tell them to stand away on the sidewalk. I make small, friendly talk about the weather and sports.

"All right, guys, stay out of trouble and take it easy."

"You too, Officer," they say.

I pull the bike out of the trunk, get back into the car. I tell the kid I am going to warn him and he can go. Grateful, he gets on the bike, rides away slowly on the street.

I measure the sound of my voice. I have shed the silence I adopted since roll call. This kid is listening to me. I am making sense to him. I could go on talking all afternoon, hubris getting the better of me. I recall how many times my arguments in the city could not get anyone's attention, could not persuade them of anything. Now I guide my speech with confidence, using only what is around me. All I need is a fucking bike.

Then I remind myself that it is property and money that forms my leverage, not the law. We make misdemeanor arrests, and the offenders hardly care. They sit in the processing rooms, cursing us, never shutting up, knowing they will be out in a few hours, for the city long ago gave up on holding them. All they will need to get out is their signature, the value of which is nonexistent. At court, almost all their cases are dismissed. The witnesses do not want to take a day off work or spend the morning sitting there. If we, the cops, are the complainants, the state's attorneys remind us it is only a misdemeanor charge and either they want to drop it or make some plea with little penalty. But when the offenders are driving a car, we let them know the city allows us to impound it. Their cockiness turns to panic as we describe this leverage to them, their curses turning to "sir" and "ma'am." Only on felonies do they listen, only then, with the threat of jail, does the law still hold leverage. I will explain to Joe that the gangbangers did not care about us, did not shut up until we threatened them with taking their stolen bike. I wish it were otherwise. I wish there were more power to the law, but even so, I'll take it.

"That was a good stop," I tell Joe, who nods.

The sixty-five feet of curb space in front of the Allerton Hotel on Huron Street was the first leverage I ever had in the city, my job as a doorman to run this busy corner in the heart of the city's Gold Coast. The old bell captain, Jeff, told me that despite the city signs declaring parking illegal there, I should not worry about it. *Park cars there for tips*, he told me. The corner was mine because the hotel needed the space and the owners had a good relationship with the beat cops, who happily visited the general manager one week before the annual Christmas party. The first few times I parked cars in front, I cringed each time a squad car rolled by, but they never stopped, never said a thing. I walked around the Gold Coast, Streeterville, saw doormen everywhere lining up cars with impunity, saw them collect ten dollars per car. I opened for business, and the North Shore ladies rolled up in Jaguars, Mercedes, Cadillacs. How did they know to approach me? They handed me the keys, said they would be back in a half hour. I stood watching the cars anxiously as three hours rolled by, certain of at least a ten-spotter. When they returned, they handed me two dollars, said thank you, and drove off.

Jeff watched it all with a blank, unsympathetic stare. He finally put his hands to his side in a pleading gesture and said, "But, Preib, you let them. It's your corner."

Yeah.

The following day I waited for the North Shore ladies, took their keys. I practiced my speech for an hour, how to hold my body confidently. I held the keys away when one approached.

"Ma'am, the going rate to park is ten dollars. If you don't think that's fair, I can suggest the parking lot next door, but they will charge you thirty dollars for the same period of time and you'll have to wait for them to retrieve your car, so ten dollars is really more than fair."

I waited for the outburst, a demand to speak to a cop or my boss. She smiled, reached in a purse lined with fresh twenties that stuck together, rubbed one off, handed it to me, then thanked me. She parked with me every weekend for two years, brought me a present at Christmas.

When tourists and conventioneers arrived in taxicabs or shuttle buses, I started a conversation with them, asked how their ride from the airport was. Many complained the drivers could not speak English, the cabs were filthy. They complained the drivers took long routes to raise the rates.

"Oh, jeez, you don't have to put up with that," I said. "I wish you had spoken to me first. I'll tell you what. I can get you a ride to the airport in a new Lincoln Town Car for only five dollars more than cab fare. I'll have the driver here waiting for you."

"Really? That would be great," they said.

They'd give me their information. I would call one of the limo drivers. They waited outside and when the guest arrived, the limo driver would slip me the extra five, my cut. The guest, grateful, slipped me another five. Ten bucks, the easy way.

Housekeepers stopped outside the hotel when I was working and asked me questions about their benefits and the union contract. I started calling down to the union on their behalf and wrote some grievances for them. A few times I went down to the union hall at Van Buren and Dearborn, tried to ask some basic questions about the contract. About the same time, I noticed the union was often mentioned in the paper. In my seventh year as a doorman, these investigations gained momentum. A report written after a two-year investigation by feds preceded an actual takeover of the union by the Department of Labor, the report citing organized crime associations, crooked elections, phony jobs at the union, and the head of the union paying himself more than a quarter million while the members remained among the lowest paid in the country, with little pension and lousy medical care. Connections to prominent political figures were revealed.

The union had run without scrutiny, without observation, without any cameras, for three decades. Now the abuses suddenly found themselves in the paper. Indictments were discussed, plea agreements made. We overestimated the nature of this awakening; the feds were only responding to the barest, most necessary legal actions against the union. We would not realize until much later they had no intent on truly reforming it; they had been culpable all these years for nourishing it: congressmen, presidents had received large contributions from the union over the years. The union had lent its money supply and organizing resources to many campaigns. But legal requirements, the rules of evidence, and the complaints of working members throughout the country pushed their investigation forward, each newly turned stone revealing another level of crime. After the federal takeover, an election was required by law. I sat at home one Sunday morning and eyed a story about two banquet workers from the Sheraton Hotel who had decided to run against the old guard, the first contested elections in the union in sixteen years.

I put the paper down, looked up the number to the Sheraton, and asked for various transfers to the banquet department until I made contact with a worker who would put in me touch with Jimmy or Pablo, the two running in the election. Within a few days, Pablo and I began a steady routine of standing outside employee entrances talking to workers about the upcoming election. Most of them walked by into the cars waiting on the curb for them, some even throwing up their arms, letting us know they did not want to talk. We would move from hotel to hotel, timing our moves by shifts. Our roles became defined quickly. I would write, churning out a newsletter every month, press releases, speeches for Jimmy and Pablo, testimony before a congressional subcommittee. I realized we needed a monthly newsletter to pass out at the entrances, written in Spanish on one side and English on the other. So after work I would take the train to an all-night Internet café, rent a computer, and begin laying out the newsletter. I would take the original to an Office Depot the following day and get two thousand copies made, stored in two separate boxes.

Pablo would pick me up in his green Pontiac around noon, and we would have a long lunch, discussing strategy and the latest news. Then we would start north of the city, parking outside the employee entrances of the larger hotels and handing out the newsletters to the workers who streamed by. They barely acknowledged us the first few months, but as I cleaned up the newsletter and highlighted the abuses of the union bosses at other hotels and described the state of their pension and health care, workers started to pause and talk to us. What they loved most was when I found out a battle between union members and abusive bosses and wrote a story about it as the lead. In time, when we approached the hotels, the workers formed a line to get a copy, and many even offered money to pay for the copies, the sweetest feeling a writer could ever have.

Soon we identified key workers at each hotel who sided with us and would wait outside the employee entrances at an appointed time, taking a stack of newsletters and passing them out in the employee cafeterias. Management often read about their own abuses in these flyers scattered all over the hotels. A section of each newsletter also provided information on rights for workers, information on getting medical bills paid, which union rep was supposed to help them. When the union reps failed to address issues at hotels, we wrote about it in the newsletter.

Pablo was the best speaker I had ever witnessed, generating large crowds of people in two languages wherever we went. He could break down the complex union and election rules quickly. When union goons arrived and tried to mock him in front of the workers, Pablo reduced them in minutes. As he spoke, I walked through the crowd, handing out the newsletters. We were fearless, the two us sneaking into employee cafeterias disguised as workers, roaming the hallways to meet housekeepers, security often escorting us out. We confronted the union bosses at the main office and at the meetings, where their supporters were trained to shout us down. Pablo would make a motion at the meeting. Before the president could respond, I would stand from another section of the room and yell, "Motion seconded." The president would try to shut us up, catcalling us, but I would shout him down, yelling, "You're out of order. There is a motion on the floor. Motion on the floor," then our supporters would shout agreement. We went home slowly each night, me saying good night to Pablo and walking up my stairs carefully. I turned on the lights before entering, visually sweeping each room.

The old guard focused intensely on the election rules, maneuvering for a way to steal as many votes as they could. They opted for many voting sites scattered about the city and suburbs, knowing that monitoring such a vast system would be impossible for us. Their voting rolls were intentionally inaccurate in the hope that one person could vote at several different sites or could vote under another person's name. Each side would be allowed monitors, but with so many sites, only someone with deep pockets could provide the necessary oversight. They rented vans, brought in dozens of members from the International Union who were long experienced at running crooked elections. As an overseer, they hired a prominent lawyer who had made a name writing articles and a book about labor unions. The bosses intimidated this lawyer so badly that few election rules were enforced. The bosses were free to flood work sites with hired organizers and pay off charismatic workers. About midway through the campaign, a new guy started showing up at all our meetings, a doorman on the North Side. He was black and a good speaker. Many people were telling us there weren't enough black people on our slate; some of the black workers were offended and wouldn't support us. This guy knew the issues inside and out and asked to be on our slate, promising a good turnout at his hotel. We signed him on. Two days later when we went to the hotels, there was a flyer with his mug shot on it and a rap sheet saying he had been arrested on several felony charges, including attempted murder and rape. He was a career criminal and had been planted by the old guard. The housekeepers swarmed us with copies of the flyer, asking us if he was on our slate, suddenly terrified of who we were. We never saw him again.

The old guard, sensing they could lose, flooded crucial work sites where they hoped we would not be. Armed with the federal reports, newsletters, a mountain of facts, Pablo, and arguments we had honed from months of campaigning, we often humiliated them in front of the workers, quoting their salaries and the federal reports of their mismanagement. We had lookouts at every hotel, who would call us when the old guard arrived, and we relocated there. One day we miscalculated, thinking they were heading for the Sheraton Hotel. Everyone went there except me. I was supposed to work the Hyatt, passing out a new newsletter. When I arrived, there were twenty to thirty opponents there, including the president, and I was alone against all of them. They shouted me down, whispered threats as I walked from table to table in the employee cafeteria, told me I was doomed after the election. But I held my own against them and the workers listened to me. In time, they waved off the president from even approaching their table with insults and condemnation.

On election day the bosses brought in dozens of goons who stood by at the election sites, grabbed the housekeepers, most of whom did not speak English, walked them to the booths, and pulled the levers for their slate, telling the housekeepers they had voted for us. We supplied the Department of Labor with witnesses and evidence of the stolen election. Many offenders even came forward and provided statements after we spoke to them, regretting what they had done. Nothing came of it. Our complaints were swept under their federal rugs. If the feds called one election unfair, we figured, union elections would be decertified all over the country, because it's just how elections work. It is how the same union bosses stay in power year after year, then have their offspring move into their positions when they retire or go to jail. For the feds, it was better to let sleeping dogs lie.

I stood outside the employee entrance of the Hilton Hotel in the late afternoon of election day. I was getting the last campaigning in, hoping to snare a few hundred more votes. Our supporters—banquet waiters, housekeepers, bellmen, housemen, and bartenders—were divided into teams of three working each hotel, staying in contact through cell phones. We had been up for twenty straight hours now, our voices almost gone, and we stood on the sidewalks with the summer heat weighing on us, handing out the flyers instructing workers how to vote. We were funded by whatever all of us could contribute, the hat passed every few days when we gathered in coffee shops. I carried a huge backpack, stuffed with campaign literature, newspaper articles, and laws governing union elections. My bike was locked to a parking sign a few feet away, ready in case I needed to hit another hotel. We started getting phone calls from our few monitors about being avalanched at work sites where the old-guard supporters were walking people into the voting booths by the dozens, pulling the levers. Retirees who worked part-time for the company conducting the elections just stared and did nothing.

After campaigning, I worked at my hotel the afternoon of the election, using that shift to get all our members to the polls. Too exhausted, I got off when the polls closed, walked to the bar across the street, ordered twenty hot wings, drank eight beers, and stumbled home. I figured if we won, someone would have found me. I could not sleep because the wings and beer gave me heartburn. In the morning, there were several messages on my cell phone from the papers asking for a comment.

The leverage found in the city is not random; it is closely allied to one's character and, therefore, one's fate. We are all of us, the camera people and the cops, choosing our leverage, and, in doing so, we are re-creating the city and ourselves. I don't know what will happen to Joe. I don't know where these skills will take him. I am not certain where I am heading myself, but I sense he will, like me, move deeper into the law as a leverage less base and vulgar, one more worthy than any others in the city, including those adopted by the camera people. I cease talking boastfully to Joe. I better shut up. There are so many kinds of leverage in the city, with so many attendant mental states, many of them delusional. Like me teaching Joe the dying art of being a cop in front of hostile cameras? I ask myself. I once believed all leverage in the city worked against me, reduced me for reasons I could never set out: doorman, loser of union elections, beat cop, now older and middle-aged, a back aching from a bad call at a mob action and the fall down a flight of stairs. But I don't feel that way anymore. Now I think I was only waiting for the right leverage to come along, when I was finally ready.

Once again, it is pointless to tell these things to Joe. Better to show him. He can take it from there, take it as far as he wants. It is pointless to tell him, or any partners, that I love the law because it is alive and I have cultivated it. The law takes me to the dead things but does not leave me there, and allows me to manage the things that do not matter. I have moved toward it from many false starts, a foolish adherence to false principles. I despise the former sound of my high-minded claims of what the city should be. The law binds the city, not simply as elements of crime or forms of administration, but because it is the sole creation of the city, impenetrable by outsiders. It provides distance from things and a measure of them, so that even if the city is dead (as I often suspect) and I have made my home within a delusion, the law makes the city compelling, my sense of it relevant. I am not lost in myself. I can't be. We provide essential services. People call us. It is they who cannot live without us. It is we who have surrendered to the law, we who know, at the top of our game, that the law holds an elegant mystery and abiding hope.

I look back at my own varying states of mind, before and after the law, and its connection to my intent and acts. Thank God for all my failures that led me here and not to the places where the camera people linger. Thank God for the doorman job, for all the abuse on street corners, from cabdrivers, yuppies, aristocrats. I am so grateful for this leverage. In it, I hardly recognize the person I once was. I maintained my literacy, studied history and foreign languages, cited my claims with footnotes and references. In those mental states I would have installed the cameras myself and hated what I have now become. To hell with that. Better to be annihilated every day by something compelling than to be self-satisfied. Finding that self-destruction is the key, and the hubris of one's pretenses can be a fatal distraction. Everyone, at some point, works in the service industry.

We get a few calls before we go eat lunch, and I let Joe talk us through them. I'm only half paying attention. I jump in if I think he's floundering. I've told him to go ahead and make mistakes. He is already loosening up, asking insightful questions. I have a remote-control fart machine. When Joe goes to buy some water at the convenience store, I put it under his seat. I wait until we are driving silently when I push the button that is hidden in my left hand, the sound invading our solitude. I turn and look at Joe skeptically. He looks at me, confused. I wait another few minutes and push the button again.

"What the fuck, dude? Are you sick?"

"It wasn't me, I swear," he says.

"Sure as hell sounded like it," I say, trying to look angry.

I wait a good five minutes this time before I hit the button at a red light, a particularly violent and disgusting one coming from under his seat. I pull into an empty parking lot, roll down the windows, and look at him.

"Look, man. I don't know what your problem is, but I'm not going to listen to this all night. Do you need a rag or a shower? Do you need to go home?"

"No, I just . . ."

I hold down the button now, the machine cycling through all its sounds as I break up laughing. I turn my hand upward so Joe can see the device.

He curses me. I hang the button on the visor above. Throughout the tour that night we will reach over and push it.

With the advent of the cameras, I wonder if what I am showing Joe is nothing more than a dead form based upon a city that has already passed away, if the law I want to teach him is already moot. If so, I am not helping Joe. I am not saying anything relevant at all. This trepidation will take vivid form the next few months, as the camera people make great strides in re-creating the city.

A few days later, for example, Joe waits with me in the stifling heat of the interview room, both of us still keyed up from the chase. We had been called to the 6500 block of Washtenaw Avenue, a large family on public housing moved next to another family on public housing. Daily fights broke out over issues we could never make out, forcing a dozen cars to show up each time. The residents of the houses stood on the sidewalk shouting obscenities and threats to each other. Other residents along the street stood on their porches gaping, wondering what was happening to their block.

In each fight someone got beat up, but no one would sign complaints. As we herded them into their buildings, they catcalled us. "Motherfuckers." "You can't tell me what to do." "You ain't shit." But eventually they went in. Joe and I had the job, so we wrote a meaningless report after all the cars had left, a report just to document the event.

Before we left, I suggested driving once around the block, through the alley, to make sure they were not gathering again. As we pulled out of the alley onto the street, we heard a shot right around the building. I smelled the gunpowder. They must have thought we were leaving and mistimed their attack. We looked at each other. I jumped out, told Joe not to drive into the alley, walked in. I made that mistake once. You're a sitting duck driving into an alley facing a shooter.

"Twenty-four twelve, emergency."

"Twenty-four twelve, go."

"We have a loud report on this job. I think it's bona fide."

I rounded the corner, looked down the street. There was the gangbanger running full steam with the gun in his hand.

"Twenty-four twelve, I have the shooter running southbound on the 6500 block of Washtenaw. Male black, white T-shirt, blue shorts, long hair," I said into the microphone as I began running and grabbed my gun. *Keep your finger off the trigger.* I eyed my lines of fire, houses everywhere. Kids behind the windows.

"He cut westbound through the houses, midway through the block. He has a pistol in his right hand."

He was fast, but running right toward Joe. I approached where he ran through, raising the gun in case he was waiting for me in ambush. I came around slowly and wide, saw him running out the back of a garage in the rear.

"Now he's in the alley, just ran south," I said.

I headed to the alley but didn't see him.

I heard Joe over the radio.

"Squad, the offender just got into a blue Pontiac, license 263F34, heading northbound Fairfield."

I stopped running, still huffing and puffing. The air was silent.

"Squad. Twenty-four fifty. I have the vehicle stopped Fairbanks and Arthur, four heads in it."

As the sergeant spoke into the microphone, you could hear several sirens around him.

"Slow it down. Slow it down. They are in custody."

When they were secure, I heard Joe's voice.

"Squad, mobile with my partner, make sure he is okay."

"I'm okay, Joe," I said. "I'm still on Washtenaw in the alley. I'm gonna look for the gun. You all right?"

"Yeah."

I walked back into the garage where other cops had joined me, everyone still keyed up. We started walking around the garage when I spotted the gun on the front tire of a beat-up car parked there, then walked over to where the offender was stopped and identified him. He was one of the combatants, living in one of the homes. He fired the gun into the other house, which was filled with children. We found the shell casing in the grass, the bullet in the wall of the living room on the second floor.

"Do what you got to do" was all the offender said at the station when we confronted him with his rap sheet with five felony convictions on it, one a weapons violation, making tonight's festivities a double felony. We showed him the pistol we recovered. He didn't deny anything. Plus he was on parole, meaning incarceration for violation. Both the passengers in the car admitted he was the shooter.

Joe and I now sit in the interview room waiting for approval of felony charges against the shooter. No cameras will record the travesty about to unfold. It is hot in the district station, the air-conditioning not working well. We have submitted the myriad reports detailing the event. Now we wait for the questions from the prosecutor. The length of time Joe and I have now been sitting triggers alarms. What can the prosecutors possibly be debating now? They call back with more strange questions. "What time of night was it? What was the visibility? How much time elapsed between you seeing him run through the garage and finding the gun?"

"Christ, here we go," I say to Joe.

"Do you want me to find out the barometric pressure at the time of the incident," I snap at the attorney.

A few minutes later the attorney calls back again.

"How can we know for sure it was his gun?" he asks, letting me know we probably won't get felony charges against the shooter.

"You've got to be kidding me," I say.

The state's attorney argues they are rejecting a felony charge because I lost sight of the offender for twenty seconds and we didn't know if the gun we found in the garage the offender ran through was his gun for sure, for certain.

"That's up to a jury to decide, not you," I snarl back.

"Be that as it may, we are rejecting felony charges and making it misdemeanor unlawful use of a weapon."

The offender will be out that night, out again standing on the corner dealing dope, out again for another shooting. Outraged, we sit in the interview room. We risked our lives. We all did.

We go to our sergeant who stopped the car, break the bad news to him. He calls the state's attorney back in a rage, arguing they have no authority to reject the charge.

"It's up to a fucking jury to decide. His friends admitted it," he shouts, but they do not waver.

"You know what. You guys are fucking worthless. You let these scumbags walk every day. You don't even let the case be judged by a grand jury. Fuck you," he says, slamming down the phone. We sit around the room bitching for a while. Two hours later, the offender is released on a signature bond, the case ultimately dropped. We see him the following day, dealing dope. His smiles at us, knowing what he got away with.

The following week I make my way down Lake Shore Drive, then southwest to Twenty-Sixth and California to support a close friend and fellow cop, Riley. Joe and I have been talking about Riley's case every day in the squad car, analyzing it, seeing the city's justice system at work. I don't want to spend a morning going to court if I don't have to, but I have to. The man who shot Riley twice is on trial for four counts of attempted murder, having fired seventeen shots at point-blank range against Riley and three other cops.

Riley was just clearing from a noise disturbance call near the end of his shift when he and his partner heard two gunshots a long way off. They started heading in that direction when they saw a van riding the wrong way on a one-way street with the lights off. They pulled it over and as they did so, another squad car from a different unit pulled up behind them. Riley and his partner did not know the other cops.

As they walked up to the van, the driver jumped out, a dangerous signal, and started yelling at them that they had no right to stop him. They told him to calm down, but he wouldn't. They told him to put his hands on the van so they could search him, but he started struggling, then claimed he was a cop. Suddenly he spun around and reached into his jacket. Riley announced he was reaching for something as they all tried to wrestle him, but his arm was too difficult to pull back. Those who saw it yelled "Gun," and they all watched the guy raise it as the offender started firing at them. Riley pulled his gun and fired back; as he did he saw the muzzle blasts in front of him and felt the thud of two bullets hitting him. He fired and fired, but the guy kept firing back at them. Riley dropped his magazine, reloaded, went behind and around a squad car, and continued firing.

When the shots ended, Riley had been shot twice and another cop once. The offender lay on the ground, shot twenty-nine times, his gun, empty of seventeen rounds, next to him. Riley grabbed an officer and told him to take him to the hospital. As he sat in the back of the squad car, he assessed his injuries: no blood spurting out, no numbness, his extremities moved, he felt as if he could think clearly, no head wounds. The officers driving called in their location, and squad cars emerged at every intersection, blocking all traffic. Riley called his fiancée to tell her that he had been shot, then the officers who drove helped him into Cook County Hospital.

The offender was carried into an ambulance and claimed the officers were trying to rob him, a claim he would make for some time. A journalist arrived and ran with this storyline of police misconduct. "Lots of unanswered questions here," he said ominously, before Riley got out of the hospital. Then the journalist tracked down relatives of the offender, airing their statements that they were certain the offender would never do such a thing. He just wasn't that kind of guy. Toxicology reports on the offender, who was an off-duty railroad cop carrying his gun when he wasn't supposed to, were originally lost, then the hospital claimed they were never conducted. The journalist never aired this strange coincidence. He never broke down the story and investigated it. He never once spelled out the likelihood of four cops, who didn't know each other and were not even working together that night, suddenly hatching a plan to rob some guy in a van, then shoot him when things went bad. The cops' alibi would have been concocted as two of them lay wounded and other cars rushed to the scene and they would have all agreed to it, risking prison and the end of their jobs and pensions. Riley and I watched the story on the news from his apartment, his shoulder still bandaged before we made our way to the doctor for a follow-up.

Throughout the trial, the journalist would echo the statements of the defense without scrutiny, never attending when Riley and his fellow officers testified. During breaks, the journalist would sit with the defendant, shake hands with him, even go into private meetings with the offender as if he were on their legal team, behavior that disgusted the prosecutors and cops. He never acknowledged the radically changing stories of the defendant, nor the suspect character of his few witnesses, whose stories also changed radically from the shooting to the trial. Now the journalist gave way to full paranoia, the few facts he built his fiction upon now falling apart. The defense was forced to expand their conspiracy theory against the officers. They claimed the entire command of the department knew the shooting was crooked and were protecting the officers. The journalist ran with it. We stared at the TV screen in disbelief, played it over and over for other cops to watch.

I came as often as I could to the trial, sometimes sitting with fellow officers from his district, the defense on the other side. I watched the defense attorney walk up to Riley and other witnesses and begin his questions with "So you say" with a sneering, snide intimation.

That day at trial, the defendant's attorney shed the notion that the cops were robbing his client. Now he suggested in his questioning of Riley that his defendant never fired his gun; the cops staged it. The journalist was rapt, took notes. Supporters of the defendant in the gallery nodded, eyed us suspiciously as the attorney carried on his questions. Riley never flinched in the stand. Guy almost gets killed in the line of duty, I thought to myself, and must endure this, the shooter free on bond.

While I sat in the gallery of the trial, I took stock of the new imagination governing the city, what it will believe, what it will allow in its courts and media: the absence of due process, the obliteration of jury by peers, willful, malicious, and unchecked lies by the journalists, stolen elections, religious leaders with political intent.

What kind imaginations are these? What kind of absurd, outlandish theories will they draw from the images of the police cameras?

I could see this defense lawyer looking at a camera image of one police officer leaning over Riley after he was shot, whispering encouragement to Riley.

"You see, jury members, right there. There is where the officer is concocting their alibi, the alibi they are sticking to right now in this case, denying the fact that their sole purpose in stopping my client was to rob him," the journalist copying it down word for word.

Despite the defense and the reporter, eleven jury members voted guilty on the four counts of attempted murder. One juror held out. The last time the jury came back and told the judge they had reached an impasse, the juror who was holding out told the judge there was still a chance they could reach a consensus, meaning she believed she could change the other eleven minds. One older juror turned around on her and said, "What the fuck are you talking about?" and the judge declared a mistrial.

. A religious group posted bond for the offender, leaving him free until the next trial.

There are two full-time agencies investigating every claim against us, even ones made by the worst felons. We scratch out our responses to these accusations on clean white paper, in the airtight logic and certainty the camera people require. Three of the five cops accused of robbing drug dealers quietly had all charges dropped against them and returned to work. The remaining two face a possible life in prison if convicted. The cop who beat the bartender will be charged with felonies, face jail time for a crime that would never rise above misdemeanor for a civilian, for a gangbanger, and he will lose his entire pension. The cops accused of beating several people in a bar fight were found not guilty, after the accusers' case fell apart in court. Truth was, they acted with great restraint. The few dirty cops? Yes, yes, of course, we were disgusted by them.

Now, what the fuck do you want from us?

What the hell am I doing teaching these kids lessons about the city? I hardly even believe them myself anymore. It feels as if I am now forbidden from seeing the city in any way the camera people prohibit, moving me into a kind of criminality and making Joe an accessory. I did not take the detective exam or the sergeant's test. I will likely remain in patrol. I think about quitting and leaving the city. And go where? Start from scratch? I think about inside jobs, maybe downtown, working administration for five or six years.

What would I do with my imagination? What use would it have?

As I drove home from the trial, I remembered the sense of urgency I felt when I first started the job and worked the Far South Side.

We drove block after block of absolute hellholes. I told myself the law was only sleeping because there were other things first. Soon, when the immediate things were remedied, the necessary laws would be dusted off and engaged. Like most rookies, I hurried from job to job, carefully followed policies with dutiful focus. Veterans politely tolerated us, standing quietly and silently, speaking only when spoken to, until we realize we are fools. Our power is diminished. The camera people can make whatever claims they want. It's just the way the city is. It's time I faced up to that fact.

The following day Joe and I are riding together again. The summer sun fades, illuminating the trees, the red-brick buildings. This light brings back powerful memories, for the city is so goddamn beautiful, particularly Lake Michigan, that I can't help but recall things that have meaning, particularly those that are gone and not recoverable. I have so much I want to say about them. I drive to Jarvis Street, which ends at the lake, turn off the car.

"Chill for a minute," I tell Joe, who gets out as well. Waves are rolling onto the beach. Some kids are swimming a ways down. Joe walks over to the other end, so comfortable working with me that we go hours without speaking to each other. I lean one foot on the concrete wall. No one bothers us. I eye the skyline, one of the most beautiful in the world. I take in the deep blue and green of the lake along it, a phalanx of skyscrapers on the shore, confident and powerful. So much seems at stake. I do not tell Joe I feel as if I am about to lose everything, or have already lost it.

SINGLE-ROOM
OCCUPANCY

PART I

I walked on a section of Interstate 94 that thinned from four lanes to two, just west of Battle Creek, hitchhiking from Kalamazoo to Detroit. The evening sunlight bathed everything in view, a light that held me captivated. Cars and trucks passed by every few minutes, sometimes clumped in groups of three or four. In the summer, their approach could be heard a long way away. I had just finished my first year of college in Kalamazoo and knew I would not be returning. In that first year, and in the spontaneous trips I took hitchhiking around the Midwest, I sensed another tendency lingering in my imagination, one in which I found myself surrendering to images, like this evening light, or abandoning all other obligations merely in the pursuit of them—a state that, when fully confronted, filled me with loneliness and possibility simultaneously. This tendency vied for authority in me, initiating stops and starts, moving without warning toward things I could not even name.

As a consequence, I wandered, not only in the classes offered at the school, but on interstates and country roads about Michigan, Indiana, and northern Illinois. Because of this tendency to surrender without even knowing why, I was already moving into the various uniforms of the service industry, working jobs rather than pursuing a career. The service industry was the place for muddled worldviews, unclear ambitions, blunted desires, and other people who just never got it, or thought they had it but didn't: the divorced, alcoholics, the new age philosophers, dopers, the indolent, the criminal. I had worked part-time service jobs in Kalamazoo, in the cafeterias at university dorms, taxi jobs, hauling dishes as a busboy. I imagined my days in shifts, knew which days generated the greatest tips. Now that I was leaving school, I would move into service jobs full-time.

I walked with my back to the cars and trucks, and waited until I heard them coming before I turned around and extended my thumb down the road. I faced another decision: focus on the destination, getting a ride, or linger in this light. Several shorter rides, from farmers and auto industry workers, had already placed me here, time enough for introductions and short conversation before they pulled over on the ramp and let me out. I walked across the road to the other ramp, the entrance, and walked down it as I thumbed. From this slight vantage point on the ramp, I could see across the tree lines, a few birds circling above. I could see lonely cars and trucks far into the horizon.

I knew from experience that surrenders were full of burdens and dangers, without reason and indefensible. I sensed that once begun, surrenders could become habits of life. If I merely walked down this road without focusing on getting a ride, in this light, as I truly wanted to do, I could be stuck in the middle of Michigan until the sun faded. Night would come. No one would ever stop. I would end up walking until morning, a splendid ache in my legs. It was the risk involved. I had done it before. I often hitchhiked between smaller cities in Michigan, occasionally to Chicago, coming into the city from the South Side. I had walked all night many times, been threatened, stopped by the police. People at the destination would become angry when I called them from a pay phone at a truck stop or gas station. Yes, yes, I should have taken the Greyhound, I would agree, hoping to end the call quickly. I had fifty dollars on me, a fortune in the business of surrendering, so I could stop somewhere for a meal, maybe a few beers. I doubted it would rain. Many people were puzzled, angered by my tendency to simply hit the road, to head out for Lansing or Battle Creek. I sat in the university library for hours at a round table, looking up when it was closing, then walked through campus late at night. Trips to Chicago were the most difficult, the most rewarding, getting close to the city along highways filling with trucks and cars that would never stop. But once inside the city, I moved in the sheer immensity of it, feeling I had discovered something powerful and worthwhile.

I decided to surrender, smiling at my likely night of hardship ahead. I welcomed the fatigue of walking, the isolation with my thoughts, the steady pace. I knew it could be a whole day before I arrived, exhausted, dirty. I could not name why this light was so precious to me and why I would throw myself at it, walk in it until it faded. I did not even try to name it, content, utterly content, in merely wandering in it.

Doorman.

Waiter.

Bartender.

Back on the ramp, I walked past the sign forbidding hitchhiking, moving deeper into an illegitimate life. I possessed an array of partial truths for the state police, accumulated from previous surrenders. I walked now without even facing the cars, just putting out my thumb when I heard them go by. People would scold me that hitchhiking was dangerous, but I never felt so comfortable, so aware, so able to talk to people. I relished the large adventure of it, and people liked hearing about my travels. I looked up, saw the blinker of light on a large Chevrolet as it moved onto the shoulder. I smiled as I jogged toward it, my evening ruined, recovered. As I approached and opened the door, I saw a middle-aged man wearing a bright green-and-yellow uniform with an emblem for the Squirt soda company. I looked in and he cradled a sweating Miller Lite in his hand, gave me one from a twelve-pack as he pulled back out on the highway, and said, "It's Friday," and laughed. I accepted it, opened it, smiled and laughed too.

His car, beaten and old, had a high-tech stereo system haphazardly stuck in the compartment where the original once was. From it a nest of wires wound around the dashboard, some connecting to the massive speakers in the back.

He was a delivery driver, told me he was going within ten miles of my destination, about three hours driving together, all before the sun dropped. Neither of us wanted to talk much. After he handed me another beer, cracked one for himself, he said, "I hate these fucking interstates. Do you mind if we take Highway 12?"

"No, not at all."

He nodded, pulled off the next ramp, made a right, then left on Highway 12, which paralleled the interstate. He put some blues on, turned it up, told me how to put the seat back. The speakers came to life, Muddy Waters, our windows down. Farms passed by, then little towns on the edge of a lake, Pinetop Perkins taking over lead from Johnny Winter after Muddy sang the first three verses. I knew the album and the stretch of road well, and I held it all in a kind of reverence.

PART II

Fifteen years later, I sat in the union hospital on the North Side of Chicago waiting for a partial screening of my colon, convinced that the city had formed an alliance with my distractions. I leaned forward, the throbs in my gut announcing stabbing pains to follow. Three televisions in the waiting room blared a *Jerry Springer* episode about men who had betrayed their pregnant girlfriends. The betrayed women ran off the stage after the boyfriends admitted their transgressions, sobbing, sinking down to the ground. They were followed by muscular staff members wearing T-shirts that said "JERRY SPRINGER" in capital letters. These staff members, along with Jerry, convinced the women to return to the stage. Audience members watched the unfolding drama on the stage, then on large cameras when the women ran off it. They became ecstatic, punching their fists into the air in unison as they chanted, "Jerry. Jerry." I remembered that this show originated in Chicago, caught the imagination of the rest of the country, and was syndicated nationally. After the betrayed women returned, the mistresses were brought out, righteously claiming the men now belonged to them, regardless of the impending child. Several fights ensued, the Judas boyfriends smiling and placing their hands outstretched to their sides, weighing which course to take, reveling in their sex appeal, a gesture that re-energized the crowd and their chanting. Jerry's security guys halfheartedly pulled the combatants apart, then let them go at it again.

I tried to read the paper, keeping my eyes down, away from the TV show and the children running wildly among the seats in the waiting room. There was some story about the mayor giving money to his friends for political support. I also kept my eyes away from the patients coming and going on gurneys, some certainly near their end, but the dramas were unavoidable. Many people in the waiting room with me were unashamedly enthralled with the show and shared their observations with people sitting around them, comments I dreaded being brought into.

"Shit, that bitch crazy."

"Uh-huh, got that right."

My lower stomach twitched again. My routine the last few months was to eat a meal at home, then wait out the discomfort for two hours. Otherwise I took long naps because I had no energy.

I mostly slept on the train to and from the hotel where I worked as a doorman in the South Loop, making just enough to get by until the next day, then heading home. I had been a doorman for fifteen years at various hotels, with intermittent jobs as waiter and bartender, especially during the holidays. The current hotel was rundown and understaffed. No one cared what I did, so I left every day after four hours' work. The hospital was paid in full by the union for all its members, so the doctors, who all spoke broken English, ordered unnecessary tests, drugs, and further appointments. It was a joke among the members in the cafeterias at work, seeing who got the most prescriptions for a cold. Much of my time was spent on the computer at home, trying to weigh their treatments against standard ones.

The hospital waiting room illuminated a perverse state of mind flourishing among a class of service workers in the city. For these workers, mainly native-born, the humiliating labor of their trade was a step down in life. These people, of whom I was one, seemed unable to recognize the opportunities of their advancement in a city ostensibly teeming with such opportunity. We recognized each other almost immediately in our service jobs, formed an alliance and friendship that often lasted beyond the latest service gig. We held each other in a mutual sympathy and marked our various fates through the inevitable gossip of the industry. All of us laid claim to the arts in the city—writers, actors, painters, intellectuals, maintaining this connection as one facet of our affliction, a connection that we believed isolated us from the bonds that held other service workers together: drug addiction, broken marriages, lack of immigration papers, and utter stupidity. At least, this is what we maintained. But what marked our affliction to others, though, was our strange speech. They found it incomprehensible, particularly when that speech centered on our condition and our prospects. On these topics, we articulated nothing sensible or pragmatic, nothing to justify our long lives pouring drinks, hauling bags, and lifting trays. Many people, particularly our loved ones, had given up on us and felt we had betrayed them by letting them down.

I knew that many of the afflicted abandoned all hope in this waiting room. They acknowledged their failure right here. In their resignation, the afflicted no longer trusted the authenticity of their own interests, those pretenses to the arts they spouted before the evening rush, in the bars after a brutal onslaught of weekend check-ins. Nor did they trust where these interests led them, and they remained silent in the waiting room, and probably for the rest of their lives. They dismissed those previous interests—things that pulled at them but never became anything—what else could they be called now but distractions? I wondered if today was my turn.

The hospital waiting room compelled us to remember what brought us to this point, to this place. Consequently, each distracted person composed a desperate narrative amid the epiphanies declared by Jerry and his guests. I concluded the city held two contradictory impulses at the same time, between movement and suspension. The city, on the one hand, maintained an age-old creed that a life of meaning entailed movement expressing a unified intent: a successful career, for example, or the fulfillment of some ambition. Yet at the same time, the city afforded access to the distracted, lives chronically suspended from any destination at all. Its devotees lingered there in the service industry, a static lifestyle, not even justifiable. It was as if even the city couldn't decide which one it truly wanted. Toward these two forces the afflicted had vacillated. They were full of desperate forays toward right living, then stuck for immeasurable periods in a stagnant pool. No outlet of the city held these vying impulses more powerfully and ironically than its public conveyances, city trains that provided daily service to the ambitious and strange accommodation to the afflicted.

The Chicago Transit Authority accommodated the afflicted by giving vivid life to distractions, a brilliant, unassailable feature of the city. It is an unspoken duty of the Chicago Transit Authority that all but guaranteed the distracted service workers would never escape. No matter what plan the service worker hatches, what groundwork they lay, the afflicted service worker will walk the few blocks to their nearest train station and there the trains loom. The straight thinking they desire will ebb. When the service worker is in a particularly focused period of reform or conviction, it may take two or three rides over the course of a few days before they are fully overpowered. Sometimes, it takes just ascending the wooden stairs of the Jarvis stop on the Red Line. As a consequence, the service workers develop an intimate knowledge of the train lines, not only their stops and schedules, but the particular influence of the various trains upon the current state of their distraction, and, if they are honest enough, the service workers would admit their choice of trains in the service of these distractions matters as much, if not more, than the logic of their destination.

With its ambiguity between suspension and movement, what was the city's intent? We were forced to draw our own conclusions. Mine changed over time, providing succinct chapter headings for the narrative of my distracted life I now composed in the waiting room. In those early years I first came to the city working as a doorman, I maintained the city seemed to make room for our distractions, encouraged us. I believed, though I would never admit it, that the city encouraged my unworldly babble, drew me in from lesser places all over the Midwest. The city made an industry out of such hollow repetitions like carrying luggage so that the afflicted might labor semiconsciously, allowing us to pursue our babble as we mindlessly carried the bags, recommended great restaurants. Allowing us to do so, the city seemed to be in a kind of sympathy with us.

How I sought out the trains in these first years, grateful for the way they framed the city. But I only ended up riding them to service jobs. The failure, I believed, was mine. I perceived a deficiency in my imagination, one that prevented me from fully moving into the future. The Chicago Transit Authority addressed this insufficiency by selling false advertisements on the track inserts above the windows, advertisements the afflicted believe are geared toward people like them, whose minds are not quite right yet: promises of higher education, writing classes. They are plastered about walls in the stations and often strewn about the seats and floor in mini-flyers with magical phone numbers, the buildings of these institutions rising hopefully in the windows of the trains moving southbound on the way to a service job. I confessed I explored them all, took the trains downtown to adult education classes, enrolled in universities studying ancient languages. I kidded myself I could merge the distracted world with a conventional one, doorman turned professor, doorman teaching literature. I rode these trains, then got off at some stop I don't remember.

I could not determine the value of anything, unable to ascribe the appropriate resources according to a thing's worth. Even in the presence of these distractions, or merely in the hint of them, I did not know where to begin, which ones were more valuable than others, where to place my resources and for how long. I paid too much for the trifles I needed and not enough for the ones I had. The trains themselves impose their suspension for a trifle—too cheaply, in fact. Anyone can ride them on their half-baked plans. Many people just jump the turnstiles. Anyone with a few dollars is allowed, no matter how pointless, how absurd their enterprise, even the ones beyond distraction, the outright criminal, the crazy, the filthy.

I began to doubt the city's intent. Does the city exploit these shortcomings? Does it encourage our babble as a way to keep us working for next to nothing in the hotels and restaurants it builds all over the downtown and the Near North Side, so that we will never see what is required to overcome them?

Of the trains, the Red Line imposes the most intense suspension. This is the major line of the city, carrying the most riders into the central business and cultural centers of the city, but also taking the distracted to a place before words, where images rise up, then move into new ones before the last can be named. It is absolutely spellbinding, addictive to the distracted, who are filled with a yearning to pause long enough to make sense of them, and who strain to hear the voices on the train in the roar of the steel wheels upon the tracks. The train begins at the very northern border of the city, Rogers Park, where cheap rent and a concentration of cafés, beaches, and distance from the center attract the most distracted. Only the Red Line serves Rogers Park. Here it plods around curves and old buildings. As it moves south, it picks up the pace in deference to the undistracted, riders who maintain a legitimate claim to clearly defined destinations. It chugs along these northern neighborhoods until it gets to Lincoln Park, where several lesser lines merge and deposit hordes of riders onto the Red Line. This is the carotid artery of the city, which from here will run right below the central imagination of the city. It's all business now for the riders. The lesser train lines veer away cowardly from the Red Line here, while the Red Line slows as it lowers, moving from natural light to artificial. Often it stops a moment, as if letting the afflicted gather their wits before it moves steadily downward belowground and picks up speed. It stops at the first station, North and Clybourn, often too quickly for the distracted to escape and cross over to the other side, where they can return aboveground from where they came. The doors shut and the Red Line now gathers a vindictive speed that causes great anxiety to afflicted riders. If the service workers, hell-bent on some crusade of reform when they got in at Rogers Park, wearing a suit with a coffee stain, on a trip that would lead to an interview, if they haven't shut up by now, haven't seen the futility of their plans, they will now, boy. They will now. The train shoots through the tunnel so loudly that conversation would be impossible if the service workers had anything to say, anyone on the train to talk to. Light comes in from dim white lamps, equally distanced apart. Occasionally sunlight filters down from a narrow manhole above as the train keeps picking up speed. The distance between North and Clybourn and the next station is vast. The Red Line, speeding almost out of control, seems as if it will never find a stop, feels to the riders as if the trains are taking them away, getting rid of them, rather than collecting them into the city center. For the distracted on a mission of reform, all conviction wanes. At these stops just before downtown, there are many cheap bars, twenty-five-cent drafts, a dime for a chicken wing. They can empty out when the train doors pull open and head for them.

The distracted workers heading to work at their service jobs walk silently up the stairs, eye the massive hotels leering confidently and malevolently at them and the rest of the city. Their minds are right, ready for the labor ahead.

I recalled in the waiting room my own late winter forays of reform upon the CTA Red Line. In the winter after the holidays, the city is dirty, rain mixing with snow. People walk swiftly from building to building, push up their shoulders around their necks as they wait for trains and buses, and stare downward, try to read their wet newspapers. The service industry dies. No tourists come and no trade shows fill the hundreds of hotels around downtown or just north. Without labor, without even the fare to get on the trains, I hang out in a studio apartment. I find myself watching daytime television while wearing sweatpants, relieved by the plots that find resolution every half hour. These time killers exhausted and half a day still remaining, my condition weighs heavily and a renewed conviction of reform creeps in, absurd conceptions of a future irreconcilable with the elements of the past. I can nurture these delusions partly because there is no reason to ride the trains, no service job at the end of the line to straighten me out. Even so, necessary things like résumés, references, and cover letters elude me.

Sitting at the kitchen in front of an outdated computer or, worse, a typewriter, still wearing sweatpants and a T-shirt, I ask myself again what exactly is a sentence. The TV is still on in the other room, interrupting my thoughts. A comma here or a period? How large the margins? What font? My hands, long accustomed to carrying trays and luggage, fall heavily on the keyboard. All sentences appear awkward. I have no idea how they will sound when read by prospective employers. I open the closet to find old dictionaries and grammar books, wrestle with the sentences for days, tossing the failures about the kitchen floor. I dig into the back of the closet for the suit I wear once or twice a year and try it on, standing in front of a full-length mirror unable to secure the pants. I consider the ten-dollar suits at the Salvation Army.

I arrange elaborate fabrications in my cover letters, résumés, and speeches. I have to; there are whole years to account for.

"After ten years as a doorman, I think I am ready for a new challenge," I write, hearing the emptiness of it, the delusional rant of it, tearing it up and deciding outright lies are the only way to go.

"After working on my novel for the last ten years," I write, "I've decided sales is the way to go for me."

I smile. How good these lies sound.

I get to the "objective" category of the résumé for a sales job, type: "Bang your wife." I reread it, start laughing at the table, lean back in my chair. Then I erase it, get serious.

I carry the best of these documents on the train, wrapped carefully in a backpack. I will spend precious money on several dozen copies of fine white paper to be sent throughout the city. I will take out the résumé and admire it while the Red Line train sinks underground after the Fullerton stop, noticing for the first time a glaring misspelling, a dangling participle, my transposed phone number. I say in one sentence my "ambition graduated from college" or in another my "goals are hardworking." How could I not catch the mistake before I left? How is it I could not see it then, but only now? I must have read it fifty fucking times. I wait for the Clark and Division stop, counting off lights as they streak by. I get off there, walk to the opposite platform, head home in a silent rage, relieved the entire, hopeless enterprise is over.

I recounted each winter of these reforms, a period that would form its own chapter in the narrative I was conceiving in the waiting room. I realized I had willfully moved into failure and that, above all else, I loved to lose. Losing, along with the suspension of the trains, amounted to nothing more than a preparatory condition of mind. This preparation was already long under way. I only had to realize it, which took more courage than I held then, or, I wondered, even now in the waiting room. It was useless to conceive of myself, or the city, outside my distractions, and it was just as useless to imagine becoming something outside of them. The trains provided an essential service because they brought many things in the city together, for good or bad, under an equitable perspective, upon a common conveyance, allowing the afflicted service worker who brings little else with him, including his own annihilated self, an opportunity to separate things according to their authenticity. The afflicted, in their suspension, develop their own ear. They hear more keenly than anyone else what words ring false and true, in advertisements, the conversations that take place, and in the various written artifacts they bring on the train or find discarded in an empty seat. They bring this perspective into their service jobs, where, though they observe the rules of their submission to the ostensibly undistracted, they nevertheless maintain the possibility of their more open minds and attuned ears, the possibility that they are more exact. In this state of mind, I did not envy the unafflicted and could never write a résumé or cover letter to them again.

I recalled the speech of guests often bordering on hysteria. Someone didn't get their coffee on time. There were no chocolates on their pillow. *I ordered goddamned decaf. My flight is delayed. Where is the laundry I sent out?*

I walk out of the lobby into the street. One of the guests runs up to me, desperate, out of breath.

"Can you get me a cab to the airport? The last one I had ripped me off," she says, her eyes darting back and forth.

"Yes, no problem," I respond, waving the next cab in line forward. The cab pulls up, pops the trunk when I nod yes, letting him know it's a ride to the airport.

"Will he overcharge me?" the guest asks me in a panicked voice.

"About thirty-five dollars to the airport?" I say to the driver.

He nods yes.

"Make it a flat rate, then?"

He nods again.

I have to explain it to her three times.

I cannot understand the large nouns of their job titles, worn on the lapels of their suits in the banquet rooms. They boast of their alma maters to fellow guests, walk up to the Latina desk clerks, who speak and read two languages fluently, with the gait of royalty. I go outside among the foot traffic, listen to the sounds of the city. I recall the many years I spent paying back student loans, tuition. What was it I studied, I ask myself, watching a stream of yellow taxis shoot down Dearborn Avenue.

As their ear matures, the afflicted find themselves moving deeper into their own strangeness. It is partly inevitable, after accepting, even welcoming, one's failures, but strangeness slowly becomes more compelling than the legitimacy once sought after. Weirdness becomes its own habit of mind, like the annual winter rages after trying to bring résumés downtown. With unwarranted hubris, soon the weirdness reveals a greater authenticity than the weight of the failures surrounding it, thereby increasing the degree of our babble by at least a third and moving us away from legitimacy by another half. The afflicted still harbor reservations about themselves; it just doesn't matter much anymore. That would be the end of that chapter, except to note that the afflicted would, of course, remain in the service industry and would likely never get out.

So there's that.

In the waiting room, I concluded we only half believed in ourselves. This hospital was provided for us, as if the city knew we would end up here, as if the city knew the afflicted would never gather whatever was required to turn their babble into something both they and the city could be proud of, that would shut up the naysayers and impose different gradations of rising and falling.

My stomach stirred again. I farted silently. Many people were coughing without covering their mouths. A life of distractions that could never be understood was a terrifying possibility. It explained not the necessity of medical treatment, but the inevitability of silent waiting rooms, for these distractions festered in some preferred department within the body, diffusing its resources. A tension between stillness and movement remained, now and throughout their life in the service industry, from the onset of the distractions until their deterioration. The afflicted sensed they were always waiting for something to break through the distractions, become real and last for more than one goddamn turn of the seasons. They felt as if they hung suspended among the city's frenetic pace, like a doorman standing on a busy corner, or someone in a waiting room, and the city conspired malevolently in this suspension. Sometimes the doorman gets close, he snaps from his suspension and thrusts himself to something on the street, stays with it for a few minutes, for fifteen years, then returns to his post.

"Preib," they said, mispronouncing my name with an Indian accent.

"Here," I said faintly, rising and walking into the examination room.

This hospital, designed specifically for service industry workers in the union, catered to the peculiarities of its attendees and their distracted selves. Little or no attention was paid to what the patrons actually said. They were, after all, only service workers, and the ones who seemed most out of place, those obviously educated and legally living in the city, generated the most antipathy from the staff, as if these afflicted could just as easily be treated in the mental health section. All patients spent a few minutes in the interview room before they were sent with orders to a long line of people standing silently outside the lab. Here, the lab workers simply pointed for what they wanted and gave one- or two-word directives. In a hospital such coldness only intensified the loneliness these afflicted service workers had come to regret, but they could not be too offended. The hospital was free. They couldn't deny, too, that language had failed them anyway. What would they say? Who would listen? The *Jerry Springer* woman served as a warning, trying to form arguments so passionately that only generated ridicule in response.

Yet I didn't shut up. My current condition at the hospital marked the greatest productivity of babble yet. My stomach pains had begun two years earlier at the time of my mother's declining health. I began a journal of her condition and medical crises, beginning with a list of medications, doctor's statements, the facts of her daily life, my regret at her condition. Each day I recorded the instances of her forgotten medicines, her getting lost, her isolation, not getting to the hospital, my trips back and forth to my parents' home in Michigan. Each time I thought I framed the statements perfectly, unassailably. I sat rereading these accounts each morning, adding to them, filling in more detail, making connections to things far in the past, even generations earlier. After reading it, I sat down and wrote letters I never sent to family members based on this journal, rereading every word to make certain its concrete meaning, airtight logic. Like notes to the doctors, they never hit their mark. Some generated anger, some denial. After I reread them, I could imagine my family ingesting them, placing them in some afflicted corner of their own selves, where it too would fester. Now I brought a similar journal into the union hospital, tracing the origins of my stomach pains. I blocked the doors before the doctors could leave, asking follow-up questions. I wrote down my symptoms on notebook papers the first few times I came to the hospital. The doctors in this union hospital only glanced at them momentarily, then set them aside. Obviously, they weren't impressed. I picked them up, tried to reintroduce them into the conversation, make them a basis for our discussion, but they rejected them again flippantly.

"You see, Doc, my parents were born in Chicago and raised here. Things weren't supposed to be this way. There isn't much time left. I cannot make myself understood," I said desperately as he guided me out of the room, wanting to let him know my apartment was stacked with communications constructed in various formats. I would turn them into letters, one-paragraph descriptions of symptoms, introductions to incomplete short stories, rambling diatribes, looking for a way to get it right.

Then, with hand gestures and broken sentences, the staff would tell me to wait and see what the lab results came back with. Perhaps the woman on the TV show was right, best for the hopelessly distracted to simply yell them out in an audience, let them free for all to see, let the crowd pound their feet and thrust their hands into the air. The undistracted feel as if they have this right; they have this confidence.

Yeah.

I pulled the curtain shut on the dressing room, moved as quietly as possible, acknowledging once again the wide arc of my distractions, tracing the history of my failed language in their presence. Upon the first test requiring a sedative several months earlier, the nurse demanded the name of a family member or friend who could drive me home. I paused, said, "Let me make a phone call," easily composing a work of fiction. I had gone back to the waiting room where the TVs were blaring, pretending I was calling someone, then provided a fake name. Later, in the recovery room after the test, I pulled out the cell phone and pretended I had a call as I sat in the recovery chair wearing my gown, an IV still in my arm.

"Hey, Tom. Are you downstairs?" I said within earshot of a nurse. "I should be down in a half hour. Why don't you just wait there?"

I felt a sorrow all my own in the days leading up to my test. The service industry, the union hospital, my failed communication, *Jerry Springer*, all of it embodied my suspension and the city's role in it. That bastard fucking city, I cursed. No doubt it was love that once guided the woman on the show, or something she thought was love. That's how the city works, providing mysteries that pull so many in, then fall apart in view of the audience, who relish not the mystery, but the failure. What a vengeful, tribal fucking city. Who was I to judge? For how long did it take me to hear my mother's own sorrow and terror before I finally listened? How well did I hear, and then what the hell did I do about it? I reviewed my own criminality and cowardice, the fact that all of us in the service industry were suspended by images we could not quite make out, yet we refused to do the hard labor of setting them out, of letting them have their say. We let the audience sway us. I remember the first months I walked to the front of the Allerton Hotel as a doorman in the early spring, recently graduated from college and totally unprepared for the city I now encountered. I remembered relishing the various views of the city in its light, a latent power in it I wanted to harness for my own. I stood on that corner for nine years, suspended.

No one, not even these doctors, believed what we said, and so the images rotted. The service labor dulled us. My stomach swelled. I had bad breath. I brought samples of myself to the lab of the union hospital in a small plastic container. I couldn't figure out how to get it to the hospital. Certainly no one could carry such a thing on a public conveyance, so I wrapped it in plastic bags, placed it in a backpack after checking the seal three or four times, and rode, like a near-homeless man on a rackety old bike, to the lab early in the morning. I shamefully handed it to the woman. The more we rotted, the less our words held power. I sat back on the chair in the dressing room, my shirt off but my pants still on, considering flight from the hospital and a return to my apartment and journal. I predicted accurately the hospital would never provide a meaningful diagnosis. They would find a bacterial strain, some other small anomalies, but in the end they stared me in the face and said I suffered chronic digestive disorder.

I laughed.

"No shit. That's why I came here."

In the dressing room, I felt my stomach overflow my belt. I had never uttered an authentic phrase the entire time I lived in the city. This failure to communicate placed me at a juncture. How could I let these things that so redirected me remain only distractions? They must be more than that. How could I not name them better than that now? They had moved from a mere interest in my early life to something demanding a full-fledged state of mind. Fuck Jerry Springer, I thought. Fuck those people in the audience. I figured once I sorted out these distractions and phrased them in an authentic manner, this *Jerry Springer* crowd would disperse, this hospital become irrelevant. I imagined the tide turning, the opposites that could result, the distracted becoming the undistracted. These distractions held something I had turned away from, something hinting at a place so lucid even this *Jerry Springer* crowd could understand and would not ridicule. I felt better just at the possibility, imagined such an achievement a balm for all the distracted in the city. The goal was not as stimulating as the labor before me. I smiled at the notion, my imagination running away with me, sat back in the cold chair. I could hear the intake interviews through the door, neighborhood people coming in for treatment. They all lied about their insurance, gave fake names and social security numbers. The staff took the information, not even bothering to gather the facts.

Exactly.

I was waved into a room and stood next to the bed where the examination would take place, the nurse fixing the sheets and checking the equipment before I got on it. The IV stood next to it. I nodded to it.

Hey.

It winked back at me in a way I didn't like, like one of the *Jerry Springer* staff members getting me to go onstage.

The nurse said the doctor was running a few minutes late. Of course. I leaned on the metal bar next to the stretcher, held the back of the gown closed with one hand. The nurse was friendly, told me to go ahead and climb onto the bed. Her phone rang, the doctor telling her to start preparing me; he would be there soon. She found the vein easily, stuck the needle into it, and secured it with white tape. I turned my head away, concentrated on Arcadian fields. She asked me about my life, told me about her daughter. Alone with someone so caring, I relaxed. She injected the sedative in the IV, told me it would take a moment. I felt its warmth in my forearm, one that announced a state of mind I ached for, then headed north like a covert operation.

"Are you all right?" she asked.

"Yeah, feels great, to be honest."

I began rambling silently, as I did at my desk at home, occasionally moving my lips. The nurse left me alone in my conversation, busied herself about my body lying sideways, double-checking the lines connected to me and the machines reading them. As the morphine surpassed my shoulder, went to my head, my distractions took full control. I surrendered to them, filled with a euphoria I knew was temporary, false, and full of vengeance. Nothing I said was true. I listened to them anyway, rapt, and here again I acknowledged the force of the city in serving them, in placing me under their control. I recounted the ease and vindictiveness with which the city delivered this instant distraction, spirits sold for almost nothing on every corner. I had willfully ingested them as a lesser, cowardly means toward this same state I now relished again, one that no doubt helped rot my insides. What was the city fermenting in me and why? Perhaps, I wondered as I began to doze, the possibility of this instant, pure narcotic, flowing through me now and bypassing my nonfunctioning center, was what had drawn me to the hospital after all.

PART III

The Brown Line distracted no longer harbor delusions of leaving the service industry. They have come to accept their lot. They find in the quiet, wandering ride of the Brown Line and its lesser-known neighborhoods north and west a kind of repose. Among these neighborhoods, the Brown Line takes long, wide turns, as if it responds to various things that catch its attention, gets close, changes its mind, and gets back on course. The afflicted, who are generally middle-aged by now, find these long curves reassuring and familiar. They have moved closer to their strangest distractions, and no longer berate themselves because they have failed. Their train never goes underground, and they will walk an extra five blocks downtown to ascend the Brown Line stairs rather than step into the cavern of the Red Line. They can transfer to the Red Line farther north, when it too rises aboveground. When the Brown Line travels among their North Side neighborhoods, the distracted stare out of the windows when pulling up to the stations, or just after them, watching the faces of those about to board. The distracted do not need to read the signs to know what stop they are at; they know from the arc of the turns just before arriving. Sometimes they get up from their seats and exit the train without looking up or losing the train of their thought. They observe things in their repose that would have escaped them on the Red Line.

Going southbound on the Brown line from Irving Park the winter I abandoned the union hospital, snow blew across the tracks. Heat poured from vents next to the window, the train always warm in the winter. The train leaned a little left before entering the long, wide eastward turn before Paulina, maintaining its speed and gliding into the wooden station. It was my day off and I was heading to the library downtown when I looked up and saw the large YMCA sign one block east. Before the doors could close, I arose and walked out onto the platform. I headed down the stairs to Lincoln Avenue, keeping my balance on the unshoveled sidewalks, entered the front door, and ascended the stairs to the front desk at the Y, where I was told membership was forty dollars a month.

Three months later, in the locker room of the Lakeview YMCA, I could no longer deny that this daily preparation for a workout held the somberness of a ritual. I observed the individual acts of this ceremony: spreading out unmatching socks on the wooden bench, taking off a long-sleeved shirt, and putting on a torn T-shirt in the silence of the basement locker room elevated me as much as the benefits of the labor in the workout rooms. This elevation promised no simple joy; instead it hinted at a state of mind wherein previously unrelated things now came together with heightened significance, one that I realized required a new direction and promised, finally, a new perspective. I sat down to put on my shoes, hearing voices and pounding on the gym floor above, a sound that thrilled me. Everything that led me here, everything that was required here, meant I must move toward my distractions and inhabit them, a necessity that filled me with an equal measure of anxiety and fear; moves toward these distractions at other times, in other places of the city, had spelled doom.

As part of this ceremony, I recounted the things that brought me there. I recalled the Brown Line, which had taken me past the Paulina stop for more than five years before I observed the YMCA sign. Why did it take me so long to see something I needed so much? Such observations were impossible on the Red Line. Ten years on that line, I told myself, and the doomed plans to move away from these distractions around them. I recalled the walk from the Paulina Brown Line station south, then east on Roscoe, the day I found the Y. There, in front of the Y, many distracted loitered about the building unashamedly, talking quietly amongst themselves, men clearly in a condition of extreme distraction. Service jobs were beyond them. They inhabited small individual rooms in the upper floors of the building. Their presence in a prosperous neighborhood recently overtaken by the undistracted garnered no attention, no antagonism. They also sat in a makeshift cafeteria and recreation room outside the aerobic room, reading newspapers and gathering for conversation. On the walls of the facility were announcements of meetings for alcoholics and drug addicts, which gathered regularly throughout the day in the facility meeting room, within earshot of the children's playrooms, where their wild shrieking during a birthday party could be easily heard. It was as if the YMCA reached out to the distracted and called them together. The distracted only responded when they were ready for the long, hard work ahead.

The first day I had arrived, I walked confused among the labyrinth of lockers in the basement, chose an empty locker, and brought out an old brown pair of shorts that were now too short with frayed edges. My orange T-shirt with faded lettering didn't match my shorts, and my workout shoes were old. I followed an exit sign, opened the door that said "TO GYM," and ascended a flight of stairs, breathing heavily by the time I got to the top. I could hear the sounds of pounding on the floor as I opened up another door out onto an ancient gym with a shining wood floor. There were ten men in the gym. Some rested in chairs along the sidelines. Others waited under the baskets for a rebound from a missed shot. They talked noisily above the echo of the bouncing balls and rattling rims. Red lettering adorned the balcony above, announcing "LAKEVIEW YMCA." This balcony housed an oval track, tilted on the curves, where two old men jogged slowly above. Both these men wore gray sweatpants and sweatshirts, and each balanced a clean white towel around his neck. They chatted as they ran.

I stepped away from the door onto the sidelines and looked across at the players taking warm-up shots, a vision that had captured me since youth. The men gathered in a rough semicircle about the basket, grasping at a ball that fell their way, taking it into possession, securing it, finding a spot of proper distance and angle, retreating into the solitude of their own craft, and letting the ball fly in arcs that joined similar arcs all around them. They were beautiful. In these parabolas, I saw instant, compelling metaphors, for the parabolas themselves, by the manner of their flight and condition of their arrival, lent themselves to all kinds of interpretation. Each ball continued on its trajectory even when it was clear the ball had no chance, was never going to make it, even when it clanked clumsily off to the side. Some shots arched elegantly to the basket, certain to go in, but caught the back of the rim, which just as elegantly spun the ball in a half-circle on the rim and cast it back where it came. Other balls moved uncertainly toward the basket, as if they were afraid of what was coming, bounced gently on the front rim, then rolled through. But more than this, when my vision adjusted, these shots revealed much about the craft and character of their creator (though chance and circumstance also played a part). The shots carried with them the fundamental flaw or oversight of their creator and expressed this shortcoming in the manner of its path and the nature of its unsuccessful arrival. I watched as the shooters, upon missing a shot, scrambled again for another ball, made adjustments, tried again, so that when the ball finally fell effortlessly through the net, it was a rigid custom at the Y for it to be passed back to the shooter, who waited royally in the vicinity of his last success, his hands outstretched to collect it and repeat the process. I felt the pull of this ritual, the desire among everyone shooting, to master craft once again.

I remembered I had learned the rules of this game as a child, handed down to me from family members with an admonishment they should be remembered and maintained. I had responded to these lessons, struggled over them in gyms and driveways, and found joy in them when I could finally stroke a ball through the net five, six times in a row. I felt my weight, how hard it was to walk up the stairs, felt a deep disgrace and a desire for redemption.

"You want to play?" I heard from the side.

"Yes," I said, without thinking.

In the first few moments of the game, I remembered my obligations and struggled to fulfill them. In my diminished state, after years of distractions, they were foggy. I struggled for breath after just a few moments of play. Soon I found myself loafing on fast breaks, hanging back to save energy. Surely my teammates noticed it. Certainly my failure would condemn me, and I would never be invited to play again. I waddled up and down the court. A teammate passed me the ball. I stood out on the wing, alone, uncertain, and eyed the basket: too far, too risky. When an opponent from the other team waved his hands and shouted for the ball, I witlessly passed it to him, then watched as the opponent ran it down the court and lay it in for a score, smiling the whole way. I imagined getting on the Brown Line to go home. This was the second-to-last play of the game. I walked to the corner of the gym, bent over, gasping for air. One of the players walked toward me.

"We play every Monday, Wednesday, and Friday, same time," he said, and walked away.

Now I sat down on the wooden bench in the locker room, lifting a leg to place one of my non-matching socks on. I promised myself I would not play basketball today. I would strictly work out, though I wondered who was playing. A locker room door suddenly flew open, and a little boy came racing through it, stopping almost too late from crashing into a locker. He was wearing only a bathing suit and held his arms close to his body because he was cold. He turned around and looked backward, and there a man came lumbering along, his father, carrying two towels.

"Dad, c'mon. Hurry," the boy said, stamping his feet impatiently.

"I'm coming, Pete. I'm coming. Remember, we have to take a shower before getting in the pool," and they both disappeared in the direction of the pool, the boy running in front.

I stood up, checked the fit of my shoes, then walked up the stairs intent on the aerobic room, passing through the gym first. At center court were three men, all familiar, pointing and counting, shaking their heads. One spotted me and raised his eyebrows.

"You want to play?"

"No, just gonna work out," I said.

"C'mon, man, we need a tenth."

I saw the gravity of their predicament. Nine lives hinged on me. "All right."

I stood away from the basket, letting a player on the other team choose to guard me, a younger, regular player. With little discussion, the ball was thrown to the top, checked, and people began moving, pressing bodies against other bodies. Alerts were issued. *On your right, down low, watch him, he likes that shot.* Habits and reflexes took over, and I discovered once again they were pleasant. I circled the key, selflessly setting my body next to defenders, picks they were called, so teammates could score. I leaned into their bodies, let them have a bit of my shoulder. Both teams turned the ball over on their first possession, forcing me to sprint down the court twice. I leaned forward, desperate for air, my legs and back aching. I sensed the younger man I guarded did not take me seriously. I feigned off him on the next possession. The ball was thrown lazily, and even as it left the hand of its thrower, I was stepping deftly between it and my man, clasping the ball strongly as my entire team sprinted down the court. My opponent struck back, burning me twice to the hoop but missing one of the lay-ups. I threw the ball away once. But I also still saw the angles and lanes. Reflexively I shot through them every time the ball was shot, pushing my body against the nearest opponent, creating a space just for myself below the basket, timing my jumps just right and pulling down several rebounds, putting two back in for scores.

"C'mon, keep him out of there," one of the opponents shouted.

"Keep me out of where?" I wanted to shout across the gym.

The game remained close, as I felt the ache of my back and legs, always straining for breath. Back and forth went the lead. Shit talking started and I joined in, but there was no real malevolence. Gathering more confidence than I should have at my limited success, I found myself lining up a possible winning shot at the top of the key. My teammates' silence signaled that they did not approve of my decision. They were right. The ball bounced high off the front rim, not even close. But as I saw the failed arc of my hubris, I also perceived an open lane among the chaos of men gathered around the center, fighting for their own chance at center stage. At my age, I rarely got second chances. I bolted for this lane, having been trained my whole life to take advantage of such opportunity—take the lanes, they always repeated throughout my childhood—staying low until I found my position, then set a wide stance as the ball came off the rim right toward me. In their fervor, some players crowded me out of the lane, possibly a foul as they nudged me, but what kind of pussy would call a foul at this point? Some moved elbows in my side and back, but my weight was center and I pushed back in proportion. Fuck you. I changed tactics. I decided to use only one hand on the ball instead of two, tipping as opposed to grasping, a crucial decision in my life. I held my weight against the bodies until the right moment, timed it right, reached the ball before anyone else. I slapped it outward where someone on my team should be and they were, the ball bouncing into the hands of a younger, more sure-handed teammate, who gracefully set his feet, squared his shoulders and elbow, and stroked the ball through for a win.

I walked to the wall of the gym around mid-court and sat down on the floor, exchanging nods, "good game's." Another game loomed, since we had won, the course of my day taking a radical turn. Daylight refracted through the thick gym windows. I eyed each man in the gym, aware of the increased intensity of the game and goodwill afterward, as if there was among the members a common sentiment, a shared state of mind. I looked across the gym. What a representative body these members comprised, every aspect of the city apparent on the basketball court: lawyers, cabdrivers, waiters, actors, musicians, teachers, unemployed dope smokers, whites, blacks, Latinos. There was Marvin, red-eyed from smoking weed, still arguing a call from the game; Mike the gentle giant, hands of stone on the court, who advocated new age remedies for every modern problem; his friend Jon, a stand-out player on the court, huge but nimble, balanced and graceful, who shared Mike's new age philosophies, studying them in the mornings in his storefront apartment under the Irving Park L tracks. Jon played college baseball, now drove a cab in the evenings; Kevin the Irish salesman with a vast territory to cover in the Midwest, who spent his games at the top of the key, where, like a machine on a good day, he could shed the slowness and weight accumulated too swiftly for his age by squaring up long arcing shots that fell right through the center of the basket. There was Dennis, a revered jazz musician with time to chisel his body regularly in the weight room, who developed probably the best inside game at the Y. No one could stop his hook shot when he was on. There was Matt the fireman, who circled the key like an opportunistic rat, whereupon he launched his scraggy shot from unorthodox spots, too often hitting them, his only real skill on the court save his ability to argue calls.

I observed the lines and sections of the gym, felt their familiar pull on me and the other players who now trod across them casually, launching practice shots while holding conversations. I perceived the origins of a measure in these lines, a measure I admitted I needed desperately after whatever I had become, or not become, in the city. I perceived, for the first time, really, that this measure pervaded the Y, in varying degrees and forms, from the lines painted across the gym floor, many of which I did not understand, to the four floors of residents living in rooms above the facility. As Marvin continued arguing the call from the previous game, I decided this measure was authentic. I confessed that I formed much of my self-conception from these contests, my age, function, vitality, the quickness of my step, my willingness to charge to the middle. It was one of these fundamental questions of self Marvin was posing in his tirade that very moment, ostensibly arguing whether the ball was in court, but pleading with himself and everyone in the gym that he had not really slowed so much. Every player gave him his space, for they knew as well as he did, from the desperation of his voice, that his claims were empty.

I saw that play and gamesmanship, serving their own purpose, were prelude to a larger measure looming at the Y. Those lingering in its greatest sweep were easy enough to spot. These men made the Y their home. They hung about the facility as ghosts, sitting on benches in front of the Y in warm weather, in the cafeteria during the winter. No one could enter or leave the building without encountering them. Many wore long beards and stared intently, looking like either prophets or lunatics. A few of these residents utilized their free membership to the gym and worked out quietly, given a wide, polite berth by the members. Some attended daily meetings for Alcoholics Anonymous in the basement meeting room, wrote down the information from posters citing help for drug addicts and compulsive gamblers, a list of shelters that provided free meals. Many employees at the Y were also residents or they lived nearby in the basement of a relative's building. All of them moved toward the Y's measure in their own capacity, in their own time. This pursuit pervaded the Y, imbued all activities there with a ritualistic somberness, one that, above all else, required a separation of distractions between the worldly and the sacred. The worldly ones went quickly; the Y did not accept them. Once separated out, the more valuable ones, the sacred, moved to the forefront.

Lost in a reverie, even after the subsequent and final game before everyone grabbed their sweats and went home, I went back to my locker and grabbed my iPod, pushed the play button right before I ascended the stairs, and opened the door to the gym, hearing the first few measures of the second movement of Bach's Concerto No. 5 for Harpsichord in F Minor. I knew it well. The harpsichord, middle-aged, hesitantly announces itself, admits it is unsure, does not know even at its age how to form a melody, almost loses time in its first attempts, but sympathetic strings guide it by keeping time in notes plucked unobtrusively. Sensing their encouragement, the harpsichord falls into a tentative melody that reveals much about its hopes, failures, regrets, joys. The harpsichord modulates this melody, adds new phrases that follow from earlier ones, seeing that the same things can be said in different ways. The strings, euphoric at its discovery, follow along until the final measures, where they interrupt benevolently, take over the ending, the harpsichord smiling.

Away from the gym now in the aerobic room, I reconsidered mine and the city's obsession with distractions. I had selfishly considered my distractions my own burden, but now saw it was the city's mind at work. For too long I had fought them, hated myself for them. It had taken too long to find the Brown Line. Most men at the Y from other professions—lawyers, managers, bankers— revealed their distractions at the Y with a discretion and guarded privacy, for, unlike the service industry workers, they postured a reflexive disgust at all distraction, like the *Jerry Springer* crowd. What a burden for them, I thought. I reconsidered my life in the service industry. Of all the people in the city, the service workers lived an outwardly distracted life. Anyone seeing them in the black waiter pants walking down the street could see who they were. The undistracted were drawn to the places where the distracted work. They would boss the uniformed distracted around in the pride of their certainty. I determined the undistracted were lost, lived in a mental state foreign to the city. I no longer hated them; I pitied them. No wonder we could never understand each other. I sat on the edge of the abs machine, seeing things clearly for the first time. The distracted life of the service worker was the most authentic in the city. The city had built the hotels and restaurants to help them flourish, not to humiliate them. The reason was that, despite all their failures, service workers surrendered themselves to a faith they did not even believe: that someday their distractions, the city's distractions, would become more than what they were now. These service workers rose and slept each day according to the schedules of their duty, which provided them nothing beyond their day-to-day existence, and the opportunity to keep alive these distractions within some context of their lives, on the slimmest hope, against all odds, that these distractions would deliver them. Their duty: the hollow routines of their service jobs. Live as if ye had faith, and faith shall be given you. The city banked itself on this hope. The purported undistracted, they had surrendered nothing.

The ceremony now completed, I got up from the machine, walked through the gym, and headed to the locker room.

PART IV

I withdraw from my interiors, leave them on my desk. It is late afternoon now in the winter, the light already fading. I turn on the news, head for the shower, sensing the approach of dread, anxiety, and eagerness that arrives each day in preparation for police work. I shut the bathroom door. The steam fills the room, making it warmer. I dislike the partner I will be riding with tonight. The squad car will be filled with our silence; we no longer try to speak to each other apart from polite, necessary statements. He will be driving, euphoric at the control it gives him, darting the car in unexpected directions, pulling over cars to lecture a motorist about proper stickers and left turns, as I stand on the passenger side dutifully, aching for it to end. He is afraid of stopping the gangbangers. They get the upper hand with him because he never learned the art of talking to them. When things get out of control, I will have to step in.

I put on fresh clothes, my blue pants first, then a warm winter sweatshirt over the T-shirt, and begin the daily search for wallet, keys, and phone. I sneak my gun into my right front pocket.

As I walk toward my car in the cold, I catch a glance of Lake Michigan to the left, see the light fading behind the buildings on Sheridan Avenue to my right. Taking the police job signified my surrender to my distractions. I give every morning over to them, let them hold me. They resurface again in the late afternoons, not only mine, but those of the people we encounter as I move through the district in a squad car. I catch glimpses of the city's deepest distractions. As I drive to the Twenty-Fourth District for the afternoon shift, I pass the places where my family began. The past, clearly my biggest distraction. I exit my car in the district parking lot, walk across it, and nod to coworkers half wearing their uniforms, gathering together with me. I walk past the front desk, nodding to colleagues, eyeing the stacks of paper for arrests, knowing they are, as much as anything, a testament to the city's illiteracy, a hopeless recounting of partial truths that will never move beyond acrimony into meaning. I am learning my way around these partial truths, admitting my failure to make sense of them.

I notice lately a slight change. I notice when I recount these partial truths, or anything, really, within the city, through the prism of my most heartfelt distractions, some people respond. These people can exist anywhere in the city, so long as they too feel the pull of the city's distractions or, at least, sympathy with them: cops, criminals, waiters, doormen, professional friends, certainly people whose lives in the city took unexpected turns here. I can hold their attention in squad cars, barrooms, and coffee shops, so long as I arrange the sentences carefully and let them find their own form. I admit a change in my mind, a belief now that these distractions, once something I cursed, are now the key to this literacy, one in which the city, and all things in it, becomes a compelling mystery I do not wish to exhaust, one I couldn't even if I tried. I look at myself in the locker room in uniform, before roll call. Two old-timers are bitching about a sergeant. I have this sense that this mystery will take my sentences beyond the endless acrimony of the city, into a common sentiment. I feel not only is it possible, it is my duty.

ACKNOWLEDGMENTS

I would like to express my thanks to William Kennedy and Tom Bissell, two great writers who supported me from the beginning, as well as the wonderful editorial advice of Robert Devens and Carlo Rotella at the University of Chicago Press. I would also like to acknowledge the many friends who read versions of the book along the way, as well as my back surgeon, Dr. David Spencer, and his wonderful staff at the Spine Center of Lutheran General Hospital. Finally, I would like to thank the many supervisors and patrolmen I have had the honor of knowing and working with in the Chicago Police Department, many of whom took great interest in the book and were willing to read versions of the essays late at night in some empty parking lot. Thanks, guys.